# Sustainability of Blended Language Learning Programs

This book focuses on the investigation of the sustainability of technology integration in the context of language programs and is based on an 18-month longitudinal study of a blended EAP (English for Academic Purposes) language program situated within a university pathways course.

The integration of technology into language teaching and learning in academic English programs often demands substantial investment in professional development, curriculum change, and technological resources. Given the intense effort required, sustainability of such efforts has gained importance, focus, and urgency. Situated in the context of English for Academic Purposes (EAP) programs, this book frames, and investigates, the sustainability of technology integration through a series of case studies of specific technologies: tablet devices, a Learning Management System, and an interactive presentation app. The authors explore sustainable integration of technology; the use of argument-based approaches as a basis for research design; and participant ethnography as a form of data collection. The book concludes by looking at the implications of the research and proposes that change management concepts be applied to better introduce, implement, and most importantly, sustain change involving educational technology integration.

The content will be of interest to scholars in TESOL and applied linguistics as well as professional language educators who will benefit from insights into sustaining technology integration in their programs.

**Cynthia Nicholas Palikat** is an English Lecturer at the University of Melbourne, Australia. She has a PhD in Language and Linguistics from the University of Melbourne.

**Paul Gruba** is Academic Convenor, Petascale Campus Initiative, Chancellery (Research and Enterprise), University of Melbourne, Australia. He has a PhD in Applied Linguistics from the University of Melbourne. He has more than 30 years of experience in teaching, administration, and research.

# Routledge Focus on Applied Linguistics

**Making Sense of the Intercultural**
Finding DeCentred Threads
*Adrian Holliday and Sara Amadasi*

**Mobile Assisted Language Learning Across Educational Contexts**
*Edited by Valentina Morgana and Agnes Kukulska-Hulme*

**Complicity in Discourse and Practice**
*Jef Verschueren*

**Moving Beyond the Grammatical Syllabus**
Practical Strategies for Content-Based Curriculum Design
*Jason Martel*

**Contesting Grand Narratives of the Intercultural**
*Adrian Holliday*

**Sustainability of Blended Language Learning Programs**
Technology Integration in English for Academic Purposes
*Cynthia Nicholas Palikat and Paul Gruba*

For more information about this series, please visit: www.routledge.com/Routledge-Focus-on-Applied-Linguistics/book-series/RFAL

# Sustainability of Blended Language Learning Programs

Technology Integration in English for Academic Purposes

Cynthia Nicholas Palikat and Paul Gruba

LONDON AND NEW YORK

First published 2022
by Routledge
2 Park Square, Milton Park, Abingdon, Oxon OX14 4RN

and by Routledge
605 Third Avenue, New York, NY 10158

*Routledge is an imprint of the Taylor & Francis Group, an Informa business*

© 2022 Cynthia Nicholas Palikat and Paul Gruba

The right of Cynthia Nicholas Palikat and Paul Gruba to be identified as authors of this work has been asserted in accordance with sections 77 and 78 of the Copyright, Designs and Patents Act 1988.

All rights reserved. No part of this book may be reprinted or reproduced or utilised in any form or by any electronic, mechanical, or other means, now known or hereafter invented, including photocopying and recording, or in any information storage or retrieval system, without permission in writing from the publishers.

*Trademark notice*: Product or corporate names may be trademarks or registered trademarks and are used only for identification and explanation without intent to infringe.

*British Library Cataloguing-in-Publication Data*
A catalogue record for this book is available from the British Library

*Library of Congress Cataloguing-in-Publication Data*
A catalog record for this book has been requested

ISBN: 978-1-032-11583-2 (hbk)
ISBN: 978-1-032-11584-9 (pbk)
ISBN: 978-1-003-22057-2 (ebk)

DOI: 10.4324/b22794

Typeset in Times New Roman
by Apex CoVantage, LLC

Cynthia dedicates this book to her parents, Joanna Joannes and Nicholas Palikat, and the loving memory of her friend and mentor, Annie Gedion, who always encouraged her to go beyond pre-conceived limitations. Cynthia appreciates the dedicated support of her husband, Alan, and siblings, Olivia, Melissa, Adriane, Nicolette, Joan Marie, and Isaac, for their unfailing support and belief.

Paul would like to dedicate this book to his siblings, Ellen, Stephen, Jeffery, Brendan, Douglas, Alison, and Dennis, for their support and encouragement over many years.

Both Cynthia and Paul would like to thank Dr Janne Morton for her many insights and assistance throughout the course of this study. Finally, we would like to thank the staff and students at Royal College for allowing us to research their blended language learning program, for their generosity and insights, and for their trust in us that we would do our best to ensure their anonymity and help improve their excellent work.

# Contents

*List of tables* ix
*Preface* x
*Overview* xiv
*References* xv

1 **Situating sustainability in blended learning** 1
 *Sustainability of educational technology in education 2*
 *Themes of sustainability 5*
 *Blended language learning 10*
 *Interrogating sustainability 11*
 *The present study: approach and design 15*
 *Summary of the chapter 18*
 *References 18*

2 **The sustainability of technology as a device in blended language programs** 23
 *Investigating sustainable device use 24*
 *Planning the argument 25*
 *Gathering the evidence 27*
 *Appraising the argument 33*
 *Summary of the chapter 35*
 *References 35*

3 **The sustainability of a system in blended language programs** 37
 *Understanding systems 37*
 *Planning the argument 41*
 *Gathering the evidence 42*
 *Presenting the argument 43*

viii  *Contents*

  *Appraising the argument 56*
  *Summary of the chapter 58*
  *References 59*

4 **The sustainability of an application in blended language programs** 62
  *Situating the use of the application in blended language learning 62*
  *Planning the argument 65*
  *Gathering the evidence 66*
  *Presenting the argument 70*
  *Appraising the argument 85*
  *Summary of the chapter 86*
  *References 87*

5 **Towards improved sustainability of technology in blended language programs** 88
  *Theory building 89*
  *Suggestions for improved blended program sustainability 92*
  *Suggestions for further research 105*
  *References 107*

  *Author Index* 110
  *Subject Index* 113

# Tables

| | | |
|---|---|---|
| 1.1 | Analysis of an advertisement | 3 |
| 1.2 | Summary of Cuban (2001) | 4 |
| 1.3 | Concepts and dimensions of sustainable practices | 6 |
| 1.4 | Major themes of sustainability | 8 |
| 1.5 | Example argument structure (adapted from Gruba et al., 2016) | 14 |
| 1.6 | Summary of case studies | 16 |
| 2.1 | Inferences, warrants, and assumptions of the argument | 26 |
| 3.1 | Inferences, warrants, and assumptions in the argument | 41 |
| 3.2 | Summary of data collection techniques | 43 |
| 4.1 | Inferences, warrants, and assumptions in the argument | 65 |
| 4.2 | Cycles of data collection | 67 |
| 4.3 | Summary of concerns about classroom Padlets | 69 |
| 4.4 | Summary of administrative issues | 69 |
| 4.5 | Comparison of feedback on Padlet materials | 71 |
| 4.6 | Summary of issues with classroom implementation | 73 |
| 5.1 | Summary of case study metaphors | 89 |
| 5.2 | Summary of pillar of contextual insight | 90 |
| 5.3 | Level-based suggestions for program improvement | 94 |
| 5.4 | Pedagogical orientations to technology integration | 95 |
| 5.5 | Example principles for blended language programs | 98 |
| 5.6 | GUIDE criteria for principles (Patton, 2018a, p. 40) with BLP examples | 98 |
| 5.7 | Example theory of change prompts for discussion | 100 |
| 5.8 | Summary of a five-stage CMM model | 100 |
| 5.9 | Suggested areas to enact a theory of change | 103 |

# Preface

As a concept, sustainability has been discussed for over 300 years (Schmandt, 2010). From as early as the 1700s, discussions of sustainability focused on the rapid depletion of natural resources that were exemplified by an increased demand for wood. Schmandt suggested that both replanting of trees and the greater use of coal as a source of energy would help to sustain forests. Schmandt (2010) points out that long-term sustainability rested on the importance of early detection and intervention measures, an openness towards change amongst people, and an understanding that sustainability could be achieved through incremental processes of implementation. Such observations are as relevant today as they were over three centuries ago.

Views of sustainability in relation to the long-term uses of educational technology share striking similarities to the term's broader associations with environmental concerns. Specific to e-learning, Stepanyan, Littlejohn, & Margaryan (2013), conceptualise sustainability as "the property of e-learning practice that evidently addresses current educational needs and accommodates continuous adaptation to change without out-running its resource base or receding in effectiveness" (p. 95). As a prominent concern in the field of computer-assisted language learning (CALL) (Gimeno Sanz, Levy, Blin, & Barr, 2015), sustainability is understood as "the ability to extend or to provide necessities and to assure continual improvement for current and future applications" (Nworie, 2014, p. 7). In their work about blending technology in language classrooms, Gruba and Hinkelman (2012) defined sustainability as "the management of tools, resources, materials, and techniques in ways that ensure the long-term viability of blended learning approaches in a language program" (p. 140). Similarly, Blin and colleagues frame sustainability as "innovations that have been or are in the process of being normalised—and thus will be maintained and prolonged—and which have the capacity to meet the needs of present and future language teachers and learners" (Blin, Jalkanen, & Taalas, 2016, p. 226). Given the importance of the concept, they suggest language programs consider long-term viability as the capacity to respond to present and future societal or economic needs within the limitations imposed not only by the institution business model and funding opportunities, but also by its 'human capital,' physical and technological infrastructure, and by the local or national culture and values.

(Blin et al., 2016, p. 225)

We have long known that sustainability involves the embedding of technology such that it becomes 'normalised' and meets the needs of current and future stakeholders, within institutional, financial, and social constraints (Bax, 2011). We have long known, too, that institutions struggle to balance their long-term viability and their need for innovative staff and technical resources (Gunn, 2010). Innovations in language programs are fraught (Waters, 2009); throughout the literature in CALL, there is a tendency to create projects that fail to achieve long-term impact (Owston, 2013).

What do we mean when we use the word 'technology'? Agar (2020) points out that the origins of the word come from the craft of building wooden houses through the weaving of sticks. Agar writes, too, that Greek philosophers came to understand the word 'technology' as having connotations in a wide variety of areas where humans worked with ideas and materials, such that the word "could be used in either broad or narrow senses, sometimes embracing cultural or social components, sometimes reduced to mere tools or to means-to-ends rationality" (Agar, 2020, p. 380). Contemporary perspectives of 'technology' provide two broad distinctions: one, an 'instrumental' view, suggests that the word be used with a narrow emphasis on physical materials and devices; a second understanding takes on a 'cultural' perspective to highlight practices that humans use as they try to transform materials for their own purposes. Kern (2014) takes up a similar set of concerns, and draws on metaphors of technology as a *pharmakon* associated with medical applications; for Kern, technology can be made and used for either beneficial or poisonous means, depending on how it is crafted, applied, and understood.

To illustrate how perspectives can influence an understanding of 'blended learning', it is useful to see how Gruba and Hinkelman (2012), for example, employ 'technology' to align with a cultural view. In their work, they seek to draw attention to the efforts of teachers and students—not materials or devices—in complex blended environments. Accordingly, they see all mixes of human and material interactions as 'technologies,' such that one is not favoured over the other. Such a wide view, they argue, is needed urge a rethinking of instrumentalist perspectives that often dominate research and practice in CALL.

In most advanced economies, technology is such an integral part of life that it can be characterised as 'ubiquitous', 'always on', or '24/7' (Jones & Sharma, 2021). As an example, during February 2019, over 30% of adults in the United States reported that they were online 'almost constantly', and in 2021 less than 7% can be considered offline (Statista, 2021, pp. 25–26). Many other societies around the globe can report similar statistics. For those without access, though, their exclusion from the social, educational, and political realms of society has become a growing issue, often termed 'digital equity' (e.g., Ragnedda, 2020), that has been long recognised by researchers in CALL (e.g., Egbert, 2010; Warschauer, 2003). As Hocky (2014) reminds us, technology use in low-resource environments depends on "cultural appropriacy of materials and approaches, using appropriate technologies, keeping costs low, and ensuring long-term sustainability" (p. 80). Clearly, sustainability is part of our efforts to be equitable now and well into the future.

Ideally, sustainable blended programs fulfil the needs of teachers and students, respond to changes in technology, foster pedagogical innovation, and make sound use of institutional resources. In the face of rising demands for technology use, educational institutions often struggle to meet a complex set of challenges (Gunn, 2010). Farr and Murray (2016) note that a push for technology integration can lead institutions to adopt interactive and collaborative applications, corpora-driven and data-driven approaches to learning, learning analytics, and tools for online assessment. Foreseeable impacts of such an influx of technology are the 'sudden shifts' in otherwise stable language programs (Champoux, 2016). Shifts may, in turn, create instablility in the curriculum and affect staff morale. If staff question the stability of the curriculum, for example, they may also question the need for integration if they cannot see their work result in long-term currency (Waters, 2009). Programs that rush to integrate, and thus 'shift suddenly', tend to underestimate the time and effort required to adjust the curriculum (Lotherington & Jenson, 2011) as teachers need to learn how to teach effectively with technology (Hinkelman, 2018). Indeed, if concerns for sustainability are set aside, there may not be opportunities for professional development (Porter, Graham, Bodily, & Sandberg, 2016); importantly, such sessions should include discussions regarding how experienced staff will enable a 'handover of expertise' to new teachers, how to compensate for the lack of documentation, and how materials can be designed to accommodate upgrades to both software and hardware resources (Kubanyiova & Crookes, 2016).

Blending of technology has taken place in educational environments for centuries (Grunberg & Summers, 1992) and people have long recognised the importance of sustainability even as the concept is debated (MacDonald, 2012). Contemporary educators working in corporate training began to use the term 'blended learning' to signal the mixes in their coaching, mentoring, online interactions, and face-to-face activities (Thorne, 2003). Those who advocate blended approaches often seek the 'middle ground' of technology use rather than an all-encompassing view (Welker & Berardino, 2005). Significantly, those working in the middle ground see little value in comparing one mode over an other, perhaps in an attempt to minimise the view that technology use in and of itself is superior (Garrison & Vaughan, 2008). In their early review, Oliver and Trigwell (2005) argued that concepts inherent in the area of blended learning were "ill-defined and inconsistently used" to the point that attempts to frame the emerging area were "incoherent or redundant" (p. 24) and thus undermined its potential to be the basis of complex educational programs. As educators gained experience and sophistication, blended learning is now seen to be a mature area of research and teaching (see, for example, Stein & Graham, 2020; Jones & Sharma, 2021).

The term 'blended learning' has certainly been debated. Many researchers suggest that blended learning be simply defined as the integration of online and face-to-face learning (Gleason, 2013; Graham, Woodfield, & Harrison, 2013). In an echo of Oliver and Trigwell (2005), there remains little consensus on what components are to blended, where the division of time between online and face-to-face learning may lie, or how differing amounts of technology usage affect pedagogical quality (Porter et al., 2016). For example, technology integration could mean simply converting printed versions of documents into PDF files (Niederhauser et al., 2018), incorporating learning management systems (LMS) into the curriculum (Stern & Willits, 2011; Zanjani, Edwards, Nykvist, & Geva, 2017), or making use of electronic devices in the classroom (Engin & Donanci, 2015; Green, Naidoo, Olminkhof, & Dyson, 2016).

For many language educators, the term 'blended language learning' is linked to the field of computer assisted language learning (CALL) (Neumeier, 2005; McDonald, 2014); strictly speaking, each term has a different orientation to language learning. As Hinkelman (2018) explains, those who adopt a 'blended' view may align themselves with socio-cognitive perspectives, and those who align with CALL tend to stress the psycholinguistic views of learning (Healey, 2016; Hubbard & Levy, 2016). Clearly, 'blended language learning' is now a distinct area, as the production of books such as those by Sharma and Barret (2007), Nicolson, Murphy, and Southgate (2012), Gruba and Hinkelman (2012), and Carrasco and Johnson (2015) attest. For Grgurovic (2017), blended approaches will increase to become "the preferred approach to language teaching and learning in the future" (p. 164) as technology usage increases. Continued interest in the field can be shown in the production of an edited volume by McCarthy (2016), and a range of books on blended language learning such as those by Anderson (2018), Hinkelman (2018), and Mizza and Rubio (2020). Debates, however,

xiv  *Preface*

about the utility of the term will continue: as Godwin-Jones (2020) has recently suggested, it is now time to abandon the term 'blended learning' and move to perspectives that see language classrooms as 'porous' environments that are characterised by fluid and interchangable uses of technology.

In light of such debates, we follow Garrett (2009) whose definition of CALL as "the full integration of technology into language learning" that operates within "a dynamic complex in which technology, theory, and pedagogy are inseparably interwoven" (pp. 719–720) to situate us in CALL, blended language learning, and emerging porous environments. Working within this 'dynamic complex', our study is motivated by an ever-increasing need to take sustainability seriously (Blin et al., 2016; Gruba, Cardenas-Claros, Suvorov, & Rick, 2016) and further examine the concept in ways that improve technology integration throughout a range of contemporary language learning programs.

## Overview

Formally, the aim of our study is to investigate the sustainability of blended language programs. To achieve this aim, we conducted a longitudinal, single-site ethnographic investigation over four years, from 2016 through 2019.The site of our study was an English for Academic Purposes (EAP) program that was part of an institution ('Royal College', a psuedonym). We chose to study at the site because of its long-term emphasis in promoting blended learning and teaching, its large international student enrolment, and our own access to the site as a source of data collection. Before the study, Paul had acted as an occasional advisor to the organisation when it first made a commitment to educational technology. When Cynthia began work there, we gained permission to research technology integration there. Each party agreed to a range of confidentiality arrangements ahead of the formal approval of our human research ethics application.

Our study uses an ethnographic approach that aligns with Kawamura (2006), who regards language programs as 'cultures' that are complete with their own histories, structures, and ways of doing things (Gleason, 2014; Norris, 2016). We also see that our work resonates with aspects of participatory action research (Patton, 2015; Somekh, 2006). The bulk of our data collection comes from the efforts of Cynthia, who embedded herself in the pathways course as an instructor, colleague, and team member. Holding both insider (data-driven) and outsider (researcher) perspectives (Merriam, 2009), Cynthia gathered data in reflective journals, field notes, semi-structured interviews, and document analysis.

After data collection, we worked together to analyse the data. Our central conceptual framework for analysis was based on the work of Blin et al. (2016) that itself is structured amongst four pillars: (1) environments and tools for learning, (2) pedagogical and professional development, (3) community and knowledge building, and (4) organisational structures learning. We also used an argument-based approach to structure our planning and analysis (Gruba et al., 2016) that drew on concepts from the three-tiered model of transdisciplinary second language acquisition (SLA) (Douglas Fir Group, 2016). In their model, the SLA experts propose that language research be framed by macro, meso, and micro levels: at the macro level, ideological beliefs come to the fore; at the meso level, social structures can be considered; at the micro level, attention turns to the use of semiotic resources in social and classroom interactions. In this study, our work focuses on meso-level concerns at the program level.

Although our work here concerns technology integration, we hope that language professional can transfer many of the concepts to areas such as curriculum design, materials development, professional development, and program management. Our book, we hope, can be used by both graduate and experienced researchers with interests in blended language learning, program evaluators who can gain insights into what elements influence success, and program administrators and leaders who require a better understanding of the concepts that surround technology integration.

The book is organised into five chapters. To establish a conceptual framework, the first chapter situates sustainability in the context of educational technology, synthesises key studies in the field, and sets out areas of blended language learning. In the same chapter, we also detail the site of our study, an English for Academic Purposes program, and set out our methods for data collection and analysis. Significantly, our work centres on four pillars of sustainability—environments and tools for learning, community and knowledge building, pedagogical and professional development, and organisational structures (Blin et al., 2016). Grounded in these pillars, Chapter 2 interrogates the sustainable integration of technology as a device. In Chapter 3, we then explore a view of technology as a system to show how a learning management system (LMS) was used by program staff as a place of technology integration. In Chapter 4, we focus on technology as an application (Padlet) as the core of the blended language learning program. We conclude our study in Chapter 5, where we discuss how our insights may contribute to theory and practice, and end with suggestions for continued research in the sustainability of blended language learning programs.

Cynthia Nicholas Palikat and
Paul Andrew Gruba

# References

Agar, J. (2020). What is technology? *Annals of Science*, *77*(3), 377–382. doi:10.1080/00033790.2019.1672788

Anderson, H. (2018). *Blended basic language courses: Design, pedagogy, and implementation*. Routledge.

Bax, S. (2011). Normalisation revisited: The effective use of technology in language education. *International Journal of Computer-Assisted Language Learning and Teaching*, *1*(2), 1–15.

Blin, F., Jalkanen, J., & Taalas, P. (2016). Sustainable CALL development. In F. Farr & L. Murray (Eds.), *The Routledge handbook of language learning and technology* (pp. 223–238). Routledge.

Carrasco, B., & Johnson, S. M. (2015). *Hybrid language teaching in practice: Perceptions, reactions, and results*. Springer.

Champoux, J. E. (2016). *Organizational behavior: Integrating individuals, groups, and organizations*. Routledge.

Douglas Fir Group, T. (2016). A transdisciplinary framework for SLA in a multilingual world. *The Modern Language Journal*, *100*, 19–47.

Egbert, J. (Ed.). (2010). *CALL in limited technology contexts*. CALICO Monograph Series (Vol. 9). CALICO.

Engin, M., & Donanci, S. (2015). Dialogic teaching and tablet devices in the EAP classroom. *Computers & Education*, *88*, 268–279. doi:10.1016/j.compedu.2015.06.005

Farr, F., & Murray, L. (Eds.). (2016). *The Routledge handbook of language learning and technology*. Routledge.

Garrett, N. (2009). Computer-assisted language learning trends and issues revisited: Integrating innovation. *The Modern Language Journal*, *93*, 719–740.

Garrison, R., & Vaughan, H. (2008). *Blended learning in higher education: Framework, principles and guidelines*. Jossey-Bass.

Gimeno Sanz, A. M., Levy, M., Blin, F., & Barr, D. (2015). *WorldCALL: Sustainability and computer-assisted language learning*. Bloomsbury.

Gleason, J. (2013). Dilemmas of blended language learning: Learner and teacher experiences. *CALICO Journal*, *30*(3), 323–341.

Gleason, J. (2014). "It helps me get closer to their writing experience" classroom ethnography and the role of technology in third-year FL courses. *System*, *47*, 125–138.

Godwin-Jones, R. (2020). Building the porous classroom: An expanded model for blended language learning. *Language Learning & Technology*, *24*(3), 1–18.

Graham, C. R., Woodfield, W., & Harrison, J. B. (2013). A framework for institutional adoption and implementation of blended learning in higher education. *The Internet and Higher Education*, *18*, 4–14.

Green, D., Naidoo, E., Olminkhof, C., & Dyson, L. E. (2016). Tablets@university: The ownership and use of tablet devices by students. *Australasian Journal of Educational Technology*, *32*(3), 50–64.

Grgurovic, M. (2017). Blended language learning: Research and practice (Chapter 11). In C. Chapelle & S. Sauro (Eds.), *The handbook of technology and second language teaching and learning* (pp. 150–168). John Wiley.

Gruba, P., Cardenas-Claros, M. S., Suvorov, R., & Rick, K. (2016). *Blended language program evaluation*. Palgrave Macmillan.

Gruba, P., & Hinkelman, D. (2012). *Blending technologies in second language classrooms*. Palgrave Macmillan.

Grunberg, J., & Summers, M. (1992). Computer innovation in schools: A review of selected research literature. *Journal of Information Technology for Teacher Education, 1*(2), 255–276.

Gunn, C. (2010). Sustainability factors for e-learning initiatives. *ALT-J: Research in Learning Technology, 18*(2), 89–103. doi:10.1080/09687769.2010.492848

Healey, D. (2016). Language learning and technology past, present and future. In F. Farr & L. Murray (Eds.), *The Routledge handbook of language learning and technology*. Routledge.

Hinkelman, D. (2018). *Blending technologies in second language classrooms*. Palgrave Macmillan.

Hocky, N. (2014). Digital technologies in low-resource ELT contexts. *ELT Journal, 68*(1), 79–84.

Hubbard, P., & Levy, M. (2016). Theory in computer-assisted language learning research and practice. In F. Farr & L. Murray (Eds.), *The Routledge handbook of language learning and technology*. Routledge.

Jones, K. A., & Sharma, R. S. (2021). *Higher education 4.0: The digital transformation of classroom lectures to blended learning*. Springer.

Kawamura, H. (2006). Program evaluation as ethnography. In D. Birckbichler (Ed.), *Evaluating foreign language programs: Content, Context, Change* (pp. 15–28). The Ohio State University.

Kern, R. (2014). Technology as *Pharmakon*: The promise and perils of the Internet for foreign language education. *The Modern Language Journal, 14*, 340–357. doi:10.1111/j.1540-4781.2014.12065.x

Kubanyiova, M., & Crookes, G. (2016). Re-envisioning the roles, tasks, and contributions of language teachers in the multilingual era of language education research and practice. *The Modern Language Journal, 100*(S1), 117–132. doi:10.1111/modl.12304

Lotherington, H., & Jenson, J. (2011). Teaching multimodal and digital literacy in second language settings: New literacies, new basics, new pedagogies. *Annual Review of Applied Linguistics, 31*, 226–248.

MacDonald, J. D. (2012). *Blended learning and online tutoring: Planning learner support and activity design*. Ashgate Publishing.

McCarthy, M. (Ed.). (2016). *The Cambridge guide to blended learning for language teaching*. Cambridge University Press.

McDonald, P. (2014). Sustainability in CALL learning environments: A systemic functional grammar approach. *The EUROCALL Review, 22*(2), 3–18.

Merriam, S. B. (2009). *Qualitative research*. John Wiley & Sons.

Mizza, D., & Rubio, F. (2020). *Creating effective blended language learning courses: A research-based guide from planning to evaluation*. Cambridge University Press.

Neumeier, P. (2005). A closer look at blended learning—Parameters for designing a blended learning environment for language teaching and learning. *ReCALL, 17*(2), 163–178.

Nicolson, M., Murphy, L., & Southgate, M. (2012). *Language teaching in blended contexts*. Dunedin Academic Press.

Niederhauser, D. S., Howard, S. K., Voogt, J., Agyei, D. D., Laferriere, T., Tondeur, J., & Cox, M. J. (2018). Sustainability and scalability in educational technology initiatives: Research-informed practice. *Technology, Knowledge and Learning, 23*(3), 507–523. doi:10.1007/s10758-018-9382-z

Norris, J. M. (2016). Language program evaluation. *The Modern Language Journal, 100*(S1), 169–189. doi:10.1111/modl.12307

Nworie, J. (2014). Developing and sustaining instructional and technological innovations in teaching and learning. *Journal of Applied Learning Technology, 4*(4), 5–14.

Oliver, M., & Trigwell, K. (2005). Can "blended learning" be redeemed? *E-Learning, 2*(1), 17–26.

Owston, R. (2013). Blended learning policy and implementation: Introduction to the special issue. *The Internet and Higher Education, 18*, 1–3.

Patton, M. Q. (2015). *Qualitative research & evaluation methods: Integrating theory and practice* (4th ed.). Sage.

Porter, W. W., Graham, C. R., Bodily, R. G., & Sandberg, D. S. (2016). A qualitative analysis of institutional drivers and barriers to blended learning adoption in higher education. *The Internet and Higher Education, 28*, 17–27.

Ragnedda, M. (2020). *Enhancing digital equity: Connecting the digital underclass*. Palgrave Macmillan.

Schmandt, J. (2010). *George P. Mitchell and the idea of sustainability*. Texas A&M University Press.

Sharma, P., & Barret, B. (2007). *Blended learning: Using technology in and beyond the language classroom*. Macmillan.

Somekh, B. (2006). *Action research: A methodology for change and development*. Open University Press.

Statista. (2021). *Internet usage in the United States*. www.statista.com/topics/2237/internet-usage-in-the-united-states/

Stein, J., & Graham, C. R. (2020). *Essentials for blended learning: A standards-based guide* (2nd ed.). Routledge.

Stepanyan, K., Littlejohn, A., & Margaryan, A. (2013). Sustainable e-Learning: Toward a coherent body of knowledge. *Educational Technology & Society, 16*(2), 91–102.

Stern, D. M., & Willits, M. D. D. (2011). Social media killed the LMS: Re-imagining the traditional learning management system in the age of blogs and online social networks (pp. 347–373). In C. Wankel (Ed.) *Educating educators with social media*. Emerald Group Publishing.

Thorne, K. (2003). *Blended learning*. Kogan Page.

Warschauer, M. (2003). *Technology and social inclusion: Rethinking the digital divide*. MIT Press.

Waters, A. (2009). Managing innovation in English language education. *Language Teaching, 42*(4), 421–458. doi:10.1017/S026144480999005X

Welker, J., & Berardino, L. (2005). Blended learning: Understanding the middle ground between traditional classroom and fully online instruction. *Journal of Educational Technology Systems, 34*(1), 33–55.

Zanjani, N., Edwards, S. L., Nykvist, S., & Geva, S. (2017). The important elements of LMS design that affect user engagement with e-learning tools within LMSs in the higher education sector. *Australasian Journal of Educational Technology, 33*(1), 19–31.

# 1 Situating sustainability in blended learning

Though often associated with environmental concerns, a body of work that revolves around the concept of sustainability can be found in areas of 'sustainable development' (Stepanyan, Littlejohn, & Margaryan, 2013) that can be traced to the 1987 United Nations *Report of the World Commission on Environment and Development: 'Our Common Future'* (commonly known as the Brundtland Report). The report outlines strategies for increasing environmental sustainability and promotes a view of "development that meets the needs of the present without compromising the ability of future generations to meet their own needs" (Brundtland, 1987, chap. 2, item 1). Other researchers focus on 'sustainability education' (Hooey, Mason, & Triplett, 2017), 'sustainable practices in food production' (Borowy, 2013), and the 'appropriate use of resources' (Jones & Johnstone, 2016), stressing the use of limited resources in ways that are socially just, viable, and long-term, such that they are made available to future generations.

The concept of sustainability, of course, has also moved into education (Cerone, 2014) in ways that either promote "education *for* sustainability" or the "sustainability *of* education" (Stepanyan, Littlejohn, & Margaryan, 2013, p. 94). As with the environment, 'education *for* sustainability' seeks to maintain the 'economic, social and ecological well-being' of present and future stakeholders (Jones, Selby, & Sterling, 2010, p. 261). Accordingly, such a focus entails embedding principles of sustainable development into institutional course content, classroom practices, and an overall curriculum (e.g., Tatum, 2013; Barlett & Chase, 2013). Additionally, there has been a shift towards the 'sustainability *of* education'. Here, sustainability entails a move towards long-term efforts to bolster teaching and learning practices, such as scaling innovations (Nworie, 2014), effective use of limited learning resources (McDonald, 2014; Timmis, 2014), and ongoing teacher training (Bennett, Lockyer, & Agostinho, 2018). In so doing, researchers investigate how aspects of education, leadership, and innovation can foster long-term pedagogical initiatives (Davies & West-Burnham, 2003; Cerone, 2014).

DOI: 10.4324/b22794-1

## 2  Situating sustainability

Building on the previous discussion of sustainability *of* education, an in-depth understanding of sustainability, and what this means in the context of language programs could illuminate under-developed aspects regarding the long-term viability of educational technology. Nonetheless, studies show that many of these innovations have failed to secure long-term currency as issues of sustaining learning gains (Stepanyan et al., 2013), institutional practice (Cerone, 2014), teacher training (Gimeno Sanz et al., 2015), and professional development (Bennett et al., 2018) continue to hinder sustainability. For McDonald (2014), long-term viability comes about when existing resources (1) complement already developed materials that align with existing curriculum requirements, and (2) facilitate students in the process of exploring how technology can transform their learning experiences. A review of the history of sustainability in education may help to illuminate how we have arrived here.

## Sustainability of educational technology in education

Historically, the 1960s marked the time when universities began to make large-scale technological enhancements in a bid to retain a competitive edge and transform teaching and learning experiences through the perceived power of technology (Cuban, 2001). Over decades, technology came to be seen to improve, and indeed even transform, the education sector (Stern & Willits, 2011). Nonetheless, failed attempts to integrate educational technology have left behind a range of unfulfilled expectations and suspicion regarding their long-term viability (Toh, 2016).

To foreground our discussion of sustainability concepts, an early example of technology integration showing how the concept of sustainability has evolved can be seen in the widespread installation of 'language labs', particularly those manufactured by Sony. Although language labs were popular in the 1990s, they have become absent from contemporary language programs and have lacked sustained uptake. To illustrate the promises of technology, Table 1.1 shows our analysis of an advertisement of a Sony Language Lab console that we found in a 1987 issue of *Foreign Language Annals*.

Table 1.1 summarises the four main aspects from which technology integration can transform teaching and learning. The first aspect is cost, where the promise is the affordability of the technology offered, in this case the Sony LLC 4500 instructor console. For the price offered, the technology promises two benefits. The first is the ease of use, where the instructor console offers an efficient system of controlling volume and related settings. More importantly, the advertisement likens the ease of using the technology to the ability of operating a microwave oven, as if teaching were only about mastering a set of controls, upon which such technology would solve all the

*Table 1.1* Analysis of an advertisement

| Aspects | Descriptors | Quotes from advertisement |
| --- | --- | --- |
| Cost effectiveness | How technology is affordable | 1. *High technology doesn't have to be a budget buster.*<br>2. *Move up to today's high tech language lab at the same old price.* |
| Ease of technology use | How technology streamlines and simplifies usage | 1. *CPU control means you don't have to worry about mastering a sequence of knob-turning, switch settings and volume controls.*<br>2. *If you can set your microwave oven, you will be a whiz on the Sony LLC 4500 instructor console.* |
| Ease teacher burdens | How technology saves teachers time and energy | 1. *Best of all, you get to concentrate on the job you know best, teaching!* |
| Comparison to past technology | How current technology is better than its predecessors | 1. *High technology also means greater reliability.*<br>2. *. . . eliminates repair problems found in those older systems employing electromechanical switches, rotating volume controls and mechanical selectors.* |

Source: *Foreign Language Annals* (1987)

teacher's problems. A second related benefit is relieving teachers' burdens, which would enable them to concentrate on the core business of teaching. The final part of the advertisement suggests that the product's improved features can solve the technological issues of the past.

Cuban (2001) studied the lack of technology uptake at the Stanford Center for Research, Development and Teaching from the late 1960s. At the time, the state-of-the-art facility included an audio-visual studio complete with technology that included cameras, video recorders, and monitors. Besides the studio, the facility also housed a 160-seat lecture theatre that was fully equipped with a large-screen projector, an assortment of TV monitors, and a dedicated space for support staff to provide on-site technical assistance. The highlight of the lecture theatre was an interactive device named the "student responder" (Cuban, 2001, p. 99), which enabled students to provide real-time feedback regarding the delivery and understanding of lecture content

4  *Situating sustainability*

so that professors could make the necessary adjustments to their lesson content as the class progressed.

Cuban (2001) conducted periodic surveys of doctoral candidates, faculty members, and administrative staff to gather data about technology integration practices. The surveys considered the frequency of use, the perceived reasons of uptake, and the uses of technology in classroom settings. The results begin to reveal the many factors that influence sustainability (Table 1.2).

*Table 1.2* Summary of Cuban (2001)

| Key findings (Cuban, 2001) | Examples | Descriptions |
|---|---|---|
| Influence of commercial agreements between the corporate sector and universities which resulted in a proliferation of technology<br><br>Need for continuous equipment upgrades requiring significant financial investment | Large-scale investments in hardware, software, and wired classrooms | Fulfilling economic motivations may not necessarily be accompanied by thought-out pedagogical applications/ benefits<br><br>One economic aspect that was not considered is the long-term viability of technology (requires continuous maintenance, upgrades in software and hardware, risk of technology being obsolete)<br><br>Another aspect of long-term financial viability is the investment in technology support staff, which can be unsustainable in the long term |
| Abundance of investment and access to technology, but students and faculty use it for non-educational purposes | Technology is used for electronic communication, research, and class preparation rather than instructional/ educational applications | The economic component has been considered, evident from the large-scale financial investment in technology and infrastructure<br><br>However, the social aspect (instructors) was not sufficiently attended to<br><br>It is possible that instructors were not prepared/trained to apply more constructivist/cognitivist methods of technology integration |
| Lack of technology uptake | Technology adopters/ innovators integrating technology through non-traditional teaching methods make up a small minority of faculty | In terms of the environment, it may be possible that the lack of technology uptake produced an inconducive environment for technology to be scaled as only a small fraction of instructors integrated technology in innovative non-traditional methods |

| Key findings (Cuban, 2001) | Examples | Descriptions |
|---|---|---|
| Lack of evidence to show that technology is transforming classroom experiences | Substantial percentage of faculty still use traditional modes of teaching (lectures, seminars)<br><br>Low percentage of technology integration | In terms of the social component, technology has not been seen as beneficial by the relevant stakeholders<br><br>This may imply that a conducive environment is crucial in encouraging more innovative applications of technology though building a community of practice and sharing of best practices |

Source: Adapted from Cuban (2001)

As Table 1.2 shows, there are a range of factors that influence sustainable practices. Why have efforts to integrate technology into language programs faced so many issues of long-term sustainability? In their research, Niederhauser et al. (2018) came to see the sustainability of technology integration as a highly contextual challenge that varied across case studies. Key, however, was to understand that sustainable practices can be embedded when technology benefits both students and learning experiences in purposeful and meaningful ways. Nonetheless, the fact remains that sustainability of technology integration is far from achieved, partially because sustainability barriers are far more complex than originally anticipated (see, for example, Singh & Hardaker, 2014). As scholars have pointed out, building sustainable practices requires support, incremental changes across cycles of iteration, and a long-term strategy (Fridley & Rogers-Adkinson, 2015; Gruba, Cardenas-Claros, Suvorov, & Rick, 2016; Toh, 2016). Although such observations may seem simplistic, the sustainability of technology integration relies on a network of components that support one another.

## Themes of sustainability

We have seen how the concept of sustainability has evolved through the years. To advance a deeper understanding, the nature of research surrounding sustainability in the context of educational technology can explored to situate the concept into a coherent understanding of the field (Stepanyan et al., 2013). As we reviewed such studies, however, we were not surprised to find a range of overlaps, conflicting terminology, and various levels of focus. To bring together our analysis, we set out the concepts and the dimensions of sustainability as shown in Table 1.3.

6  *Situating sustainability*

*Table 1.3* Concepts and dimensions of sustainable practices

| Area of focus | Description | References |
|---|---|---|
| Conceptual orientations | 1. Sustainability as an ecology<br>• Multilevel stakeholder involvement (macro, meso, micro)<br>• Iterative process of innovation and reflection of all stakeholders<br>2. Sustainability as ongoing change | Toh (2016)<br>Niederhauser et al. (2018) |
| Dimensions of sustainability | 1. Institution<br>2. Developer<br>3. Instructor<br>4. Student<br>5. Technology<br>1. Social<br>2. Political<br>3. Economic<br>4. Technological<br>5. Institutional factors | McGill, Klobas, and Renzi (2014)<br>Pouezevara, Mekhael, and Darcy (2014) |

As Table 1.3 shows, sustainability is often framed at the macro, or overarching, level, using metaphors of 'ecology' and 'change'; at a lower level, sustainability dimensions are set out as factors that relate to the concept. For example, Toh (2016) views sustainable educational technology as a network of ecological systems comprising complex social structures. Given this view, Toh advocates a need for institutional stakeholder engagement at multiple levels to ensure the sustainability of educational technology. Fundamental to this view of sustainability is that stakeholders such as administrators, support staff, and teachers engage in an iterative process of innovation which entails a continuous reflection on the implementation and refinement of their technology integration initiatives (Toh, 2016). Given the complexity of CALL environments' intricate adaptive systems (Schulze & Scholz, 2016), an ecological metaphor is useful in the mapping of factors that may influence the success of sustainable educational innovations.

'Ongoing change' is another conceptual orientation. For Niederhauser et al. (2018), 'change' refers to the continuous introduction of technological innovations that have been designed to transform students' learning experiences. The researchers characterise transformative learning experiences as part of the capacity of technology integration to incorporate diverse modes for student learning, including communication, interaction, collaboration, and engagement with authentic learning materials. For them, any effort to promote sustainability must entail long-term transition because the integration of technology into a language program cannot be achieved without "persistent and ongoing change in the educational culture" (Niederhauser et al., 2018, p. 509).

A consideration of the dimensions of sustainability helps to identify specific factors that influence successful long-term integration. McGill et al. (2014) set out dimensions that are more confined than those of Pouezevara et al. (2014), yet each includes 'technology' and 'institution' as contributing factors of sustainability. What distinguishes the two frameworks, however, is the overt inclusion of 'political' and 'economic' aspects by Pouezevara et al. (2014) that suggest that sustainability encompasses factors far beyond an immediate educational setting.

Table 1.4 summarises factors related to the themes of educational institutions and strategies for effective long-term technology integration. Characteristic of educational institutions, the table highlights the role of such factors as scalability, uptake, and long-term viability.

As the studies reviewed in Table 1.4 demonstrate, scalability is frequently mentioned (Nworie, 2014; Niederhauser et al., 2018; Bennett et al., 2018). For example, Nworie (2014) discusses the importance of scalability in terms of extending pedagogical gains, so that they continue to develop and benefit both present and future stakeholders. A similar argument is advanced by Niederhauser et al. (2018), who define scalability as extending or applying educational innovations beyond their original contexts. Niederhauser et al. (2018) also assert that scaling innovations is crucial for sustainability, as technological initiatives need constant refinement through an iterative process of feedback and improvement. Besides the extension of pedagogical innovations, a more specific discussion is proposed by Bennett et al. (2018), who discuss scalability in terms of teacher capacity building. In this context, Bennett et al. (2018) argue that for teacher capacity building to be sustainable, there must be a focus on the complexities involved when teachers design learning resources.

Uptake, or stakeholder adoption and support of change initiatives, is also strongly associated with sustainability (Nworie, 2014; Niederhauser et al., 2018). For Nworie (2014), technological initiatives are sustainable when such initiatives are embedded into an institutional culture. Adding to this, Niederhauser et al. (2018) argue that uptake occurred when the technology demonstrated pedagogical affordances such that it was maintained. To clarify, 'affordance' is seen as the potential of an artefact (e.g., a move in an application such as a change of colour) to enhance pedagogical effectiveness (Bower & Sturman, 2015; Spector, 2015). In short, instructors adopt and integrate technology when it demonstrates value to their teaching and learning practices.

A third major theme of sustainability is long-term viability, which has also been a focus of researchers (Hall Giesinger et al., 2016; Raji &

Table 1.4 Major themes of sustainability

| Area of focus | Description | References |
| --- | --- | --- |
| Major themes within educational institutions | Scalability<br>• Scaling innovations<br>• Teacher capacity building | Nworie (2014)<br>Niederhauser et al. (2018)<br>Bennett et al. (2018) |
| | Uptake<br>• Institutionalising innovations<br>• Benefits of innovation are recognised, maintained | Nworie (2014)<br>Niederhauser et al. (2018) |
| | Long-term viability<br>• Planning<br>• Personnel/funding changes<br>• Determining the most sustainable technology | Hall Giesinger et al. (2016)<br>Raji and Zualkernan (2016) |
| Strategies for effective long-term technology integration | Project management<br>• Long-term planning (clear, justifiable goals, attention to key decisions)<br>• Concern for sustainability<br>• Leadership | Fridley and Rogers-Adkinson (2015)<br>Gunn (2010)<br>Niederhauser et al. (2018)<br>Gruba et al. (2016)<br>Jones and Johnstone (2016)<br>Hall Giesinger et al. (2016)<br>Toh (2016)<br>Gannaway, Hinton, Berry, and Moore (2013)<br>Timmis (2014)<br>Bennett et al. (2018) |
| | Resource management<br>• Investment (in strategy, staff, infrastructure)<br>• Adequate support and management of resources<br>• Adequate professional development/training<br>• Balance between economic and pedagogical needs | |
| | Embedding technology integration<br>• Shared vision<br>• Dissemination<br>• Staff accountability<br>• Multi-stakeholder involvement<br>• Teachers as drivers of sustainability | |

Zualkernan, 2016). Referring to concerns for the longevity and prolonged benefits of educational technology, a vital aspect of long-term viability is proper planning prior to implementation. For example, Hall Giesinger, Adams Becker, Davis, and Shedd (2016) highlight the importance of proposed countermeasures to address potential changes in personnel and funding allocations, considering how such changes could impact the availability of existing resources. Conversely, a study by Raji and Zualkernan (2016) focused on maximising the limited availability of resources in the context of technology for developing countries. The authors stress the importance of initial planning to determine the most sustainable technology integration platform to adopt prior to implementation. Applying the BOCR (benefits, opportunities, resources, and risks) framework, the authors weighed the benefits, opportunities, resources, and risks of each proposed technology before determining which platform was most sustainable (Raji & Zualkernan, 2016, p. 310).

Studies also emphasise the need for strategies that may promote long-term technology integration. To facilitate the analysis, we have sub-divided the strategies into areas of project management, resource management, and embedding technology integration. Broadly speaking, the bulk of studies examining strategies for sustainability discuss institutional factors (Gunn, 2010; Timmis, 2014; Fridley & Rogers-Adkinson, 2015; Jones & Johnstone, 2016; Toh, 2016; Bennett et al., 2018; Niederhauser et al., 2018) that underscore the importance of macro- and meso-level considerations that influence sustainability.

To illustrate, applying a project management approach to sustainability necessitates a long-term view of technology integration by establishing clear goals, attending to key decisions, and displaying a capacity for leadership (Fridley & Rogers-Adkinson, 2015). In terms of resource management, considering the substantial investment demands of technology integration, administrators should not only ensure that robust support systems are in place (Gunn, 2010; Niederhauser et al., 2018) but also that such resources are managed with long-term viability in mind (Timmis, 2014; Gruba et al., 2016; Jones & Johnstone, 2016). Further, embedding a culture of technology integration within the institution is crucial for sustainability. This can be established through a shared vision and implementing appropriate dissemination (Gannaway et al., 2013) strategies. The importance of multiple-stakeholder involvement (Toh, 2016) is also crucial to sustainability, where key staff such as teachers (Bennett et al., 2018) need to be accountable to the shared goals of the institution (Hall Giesinger et al., 2016).

Our review shows that concepts related to sustainability overlap, conflict, and have multiple levels of focus. Nevertheless, situating the discussion of studies according to categories of conceptual orientations, dimensions, major themes, and strategies clearly illustrate sustainability as a non-linear, multifaceted concept. In summary, what can be concluded from the analysis of studies is that they are complex and inter-related, and, much like a system, "operat[e] at different levels of granularity, from the macro level to the micro level" (Blin, 2016, p. 47). By implication, an in-depth investigation of sustainability would require a framework which acknowledges such complexities and incorporates a multi-level conceptual framework for examining the intricacies involved in sustaining technology integration initiatives.

## Blended language learning

Following a review of 'lone wolf' projects in CALL (Hubbard, 2005), Gruba and Hinkelman (2012) suggested that sustainability was affected by a lack of scalability, poor teacher uptake, and the lack of incentives to build on the work of others. Advancing such concepts, Blin, Jalkanen, and Taalas (2016) constructed an ecosystem model that sets out an inter-dependent, hierarchical relationship among the four sustainability pillars.

For Blin and colleagues (2016), the first pillar of sustainability considers the educational environment and tools for learning. What are the capabilities and affordances of a particular technology, and what is its role in language learning? As Healey (2016) has observed, such questions are not easy to answer as the fast pace of change, the degree of integration, and varied affordances of technology vary from one language program to another. Further, as Chapelle (2014) notes, any view of a complex environment must also attempt to account for a mix of instructional designs, pedagogical resources, and teacher levels of expertise. For Eskildsen and Theodórsdóttir (2015), affordances of technology should stress the need to benefit students through a learner-centred pedagogy that is driven by authentic learning experiences. In summary, Blin et al. (2016) argue that sustainable environments are those that are purposeful, tailored to the needs of stakeholders, aligned with learning objectives, and foster engagement in classroom tasks and activities.

As a second pillar in their model, Blin and colleagues (2016) argue that pedagogical and professional development is vital in sustaining the use of educational technology (Robertson, 2008). Through professional development, they note, teachers can be encouraged to be the change agents of new teaching initiatives and adapt teaching practices to changing environments. With regard to training on the use of technological learning tools, Kennedy and Levy (2009) contend that such training should not only address technical aspects, but more important, provide input on the educational value of such tools and how to best use them. In other words, they suggest that language teachers would benefit the most from training that is suited to the design and content of language instructional materials. It is the lack of such training and skills that often makes it difficult for teaching staff to embrace technology in their teaching. Littlejohn (2003) attributes teachers' resistance to technology use to the complexities of design and implementation that, perhaps, is best addressed through a comprehensive model of academic support. Similarly, Gunn (2011) calls on educators to have greater involvement in the tools and learning designs of their courses in order to address current pedagogical and technological limitations.

The third pillar of the Blin et al. (2016) framework concerns the need to develop the community and knowledge sharing practices within a program.

A community of teachers, they note, entails mutual help in evolving and adapting current teaching perspectives and practices and helps support the use of tools and environments necessary for implementation. It is vital to the sustainability of technological innovation to focus on teachers, who have the crucial role as agents of change in blended learning contexts (Kennedy & Levy, 2009). In their review of successful implementations over a 15-year period, Kennedy and Levy found that successful teams fostered continuous adaptation as they embedded and refined their language learning projects. Brečko, Kampylis, and Punie (2014) also found that sustainability involves knowledge sharing, diffusion of best practices, and cultivating a 'culture of innovation' throughout the organisation. A keen sense of community, or what Brečko and colleagues (2014) saw as 'connectedness', included "the extent to which innovative pedagogical, technological and organisational practices reach beyond the model of isolated learner/classroom/school" (p. 25); accordingly, the building of communities encompassed not only teachers but also learners who sought to improve learning experiences by engaging with each other and with concepts in ways that led to substantial institutional policy and change.

Organisational structure, though often outside teacher control, is a fourth pillar of sustainability for Blin and colleagues (2016). In their discussion, they highlight three key aspects: the importance of transparency, a view of the organisation as a unit, and a need for widespread change to be implemented in line with broader institutional objectives. Perhaps most crucial as a key driver of sustainability, Gannaway et al. (2013) argue, is to ensure that institutional goals and objectives are shared with all stakeholders through three inter-related actions: 'assess climate', 'engage', and 'transfer'. For Schalock, Verdugo, and Lee (2016) sustainability depends on accountability (effectiveness and efficiency), leadership (transformational leadership and strategic execution), and organisation (high-performance teams and continuous quality improvement). With regard to organisation and leadership, Brečko et al. (2014) argue for policies which enable educational organisations to clearly outline their approach to sustainability and more advanced pedagogy, acknowledging that this may involve transforming aspects of their organisational and leadership structures.

## Interrogating sustainability

One trend in applied linguistics research is to make use of interpretive arguments as a way to interrogate concepts. Building on the work of Kane (2006), for example, Chapelle, Enright, and Jamieson (2008) applied interpretive arguments to validation studies in the work of language testing and assessment. In a keynote speech delivered to a prominent CALL conference,

Chapelle (2014) set out five types of arguments that typify claims in the field: comparison, authenticity, data-driven language learning, theory-based, and pedagogy. In a comparison argument, for example, a researcher would employ a design to find significant differences between an experimental and a control group; for example, a statistical analysis of a survey of classes that used technology against those that did not. However, as Chapelle (2014) has pointed out, the widespread use of technology outside of the classroom now all but precludes such investigations: that is, for most students, technology has long been part of their lives and they have come to expect its use in their education.

A second argument for the use of technology would claim that new literacies, for example, are now part of the authenticity of classroom experiences needed to prepare students for the real world (Lotherington & Jenson, 2011). According to Chapelle (2014), however, claims of authenticity need to be calibrated against the actual use of technology through a long-term study of actual uses in the workplace, for example.

A third argument in blended language learning seeks to justify that claim that, for example, students need language for specific purposes and thus a data-driven or corpus-based set of materials would be needed (Chapelle, 2014). For this reason, nglish for Academic Purposes curricula are built on discipline-specific designs and pedagogies that could be underpinned by widespread uses of corpora and salient examples. Despite its promise, however, there has not been a wide uptake in the use of technology to inform present-day curricula. A fourth type of argument uses research in second-language acquisition to align the use of technology, for example, to drive lessons that are 'learner fit' Chapelle (2014, 2009). The use of theory, at times, strains the ability to link theoretical concepts to actual pedagogical practices and thus may have limited utility for practitioners.

Chapelle (2014) describes the most widely used argument, a fifth category of research claiming that pedagogical choices and principles can drive the use of technology in language learning. In programs that teach conversational skills, for example, videoconferencing may enable students at remote locations with differing languages the opportunity to engage in conversation. Much as with theory-based arguments, Chapelle notes, pedagogically driven justifications for technology use must demonstrate clear links between what is intended and what occurs with reference to language learning designs.

Other studies show how an argument-based approach may be used to investigate classroom language teaching and learning. For example, Li (2015) applied the argument-based approach to a validity study of video-based listening comprehension tests. Gleason (2013) adopted interpretive arguments to the wider context of blended language course design, contending that interpretive arguments can both guide and make way for more informed blended language teaching practices. In the study, interpretive arguments were used to assess the validity of three language tasks which were conducted in different combinations of face-to-face and blended settings. Further work by Chapelle, Cotos, and Lee (2015) applied the argument-based approach in validating two automated writing evaluation tools incorporated in the English for Academic Purposes (EAP) writing classes at the undergraduate and graduate levels.

Inspired by such work, Gruba and colleagues (2016) adapted interpretive arguments to evaluate blended language programs in Australia, Chile, the United States, and Vietnam. Significantly, their work situated the evaluation of blended approaches in a three-tier model that encouraged researchers to take into macro-, meso-, and micro-influences of language learning. At the macro level, they suggested, program evaluation is directed by global, national, or institutional policies that set overall directions in resource allocation and thinking. The meso level seeks to identify the program level where administrators and instructors discuss aspects of the curriculum, for example, that include material design, assessments, and uses of technology. The classroom encompasses the micro level, where designs and interaction take place to foster learning. Of note, the Douglas Fir Group (2016) also proposed a similar three-tier model to support their call for 'transdisciplinary second language acquisition' that could be used to consider greater student mobility and the greater uses of technology and media in ways that better recognise the myriad of factors that influence language learning.

The argument-based approach develops in four stages: (1) planning an argument, (2) gathering the evidence, (3) presenting the argument, and (4) appraising the argument. The planning stage of argument construction starts with explicitly laying out the claims which can be made at distinct stages of the investigation. These stages refer to the network of five inferences which include domain definition, evaluation, explanation, utilisation and ramification (see Table 1.5). Starting with the domain definition inference, a claim is then connected to the next inference, evaluation, and so on, until it reaches the final inference, ramification. It is within this network of inferences that claims are connected to one another. Claims are crucial in the process of argument building as they map out the direction of the investigation and outline evidence required to back each of the claims (Chapelle, 2014).

After passing the evidence through a series of inferences, an appraisal is made to determine whether the claims are strong, moderate, or weak (Golonka, Bowles, Frank, Richardson, & Freynik, 2014). To illustrate, at the meso level, a claim regarding sustainability could propose that instructors have access to an online repository of materials, resources, and tools to support the continued use of technology in the language classroom. The

14  *Situating sustainability*

*Table 1.5* Example argument structure (adapted from Gruba et al., 2016)

| |
|---|
| **Broader implication:** claims showing how the study findings are transferrable to other contexts (e.g., similar programs/contexts) |
| ↑ **Ramification inference** ↑ <br> **Program improvement:** claims which show the practical applications of study outcomes to further develop the program |
| ↑ **Utilisation inference** ↑ <br> **Rationale:** statements which show the contextual reasoning behind study outcomes |
| ↑ **Explanation inference** ↑ <br> **Findings:** claims which outline what can be discovered via data analysis about blended learning in the program |
| ↑ **Evaluation inference** ↑ <br> **Data collection:** claims regarding the types of data required to carry out the investigation |
| ↑ **Domain definition inference** ↑ <br> **Target domain**: contextualises the investigation of the blended language program by determining the level(s) and consideration(s) central to the study |

underlying inferences, warrants, and corresponding assumptions behind this claim would need to be clearly specified, together with the evidence needed to back up the claim. The evidence needed to interrogate the claim could take the form of individual or group interviews with instructors, instructional designers, and technical staff as well as administrators.

To demonstrate the utility of the argument-based approach, Gruba et al. (2016) presented case studies that highlighted differing levels and considerations. In one such case study of the meso level, Rick (2016) investigated the multi-faceted nature of blended learning sustainability and its complex network of interacting factors. Based in Vietnam, Rick looked at various factors that influenced technology integration in an academic English program, including, for example, key performance indicators, professional development, shared resource banks, and formal documentation.

Using the interpretive argument structure to interrogate claims made regarding the sustainability of technology, Rick (2016) showed that implementation and support were crucial. In an analysis of implementation factors, themes surrounding pedagogy, strategic planning, and student engagement emerged. In the area of support, analysis showed the program could better implement professional development practices and recognise the limits of technology. Rick showed that, despite program administrator support and acknowledgement of the importance of technology integration, several barriers affected sustainability, among them technological limitations including unreliable technology, curricular restrictions, perceived motivation for technology as a tool for marketing and cost-effective measure, lack of teacher release time for curriculum development work, and decreased student engagement.

## The present study: approach and design

Following Sayago (2015), we see the importance of establishing a philosophical frame to underpin our data collection and analysis. Denzin and Lincoln (2003) suggest that researchers set out an underlying ontology (how we view reality), epistemology (how the researcher and the researched relate to each other), and methodology (how we obtain knowledge of the world) to guide research. Throughout this study, we view our work through the subjective lens of the interpretivist paradigm (Lynch, 2003) as we seek to better understand how 'innovations' (Waters, 2009) are sustained in the context of language programs. According to the interpretivist paradigm, reality is not a fixed construct but is fluid and interpreted according to the meaning participants ascribe to it (Lynch, 2003).

More specifically, our study employs the constructivist form of interpretive paradigm as it is used in post-positivist, feminist, and cultural studies research (Denzin & Lincoln, 2003). The constructivist paradigm assumes the existence of multiple realities and the subjectivity of lived experiences according to the meaning attached to such experiences (Denzin & Lincoln, 2003). Additionally, this paradigm does not delineate the positionality of the researcher from the research site nor its participants (Owen, 2014); the researcher and the researched work together in building the subjective interpretation of lived experiences in real-life settings (Yin, 2015). Table 1.6 summarises our overall plan.

Notably, Cynthia was on site as an 'ethnographic researcher' who was also employed as a full-time language instructor at the site; Paul provided work on document analysis (Bowen, 2009; De Wever, Schellens, Valcke, & Van Keer, 2006). Together, we intended to construct our views through the lens of the four pillars of blended language learning set out by Blin and colleagues (2016) and then consider our findings through interpretive arguments at the meso level of program coordinators and instructors. Despite institutional support, obtaining the final approval to conduct research at the institution was not an easy task. Discussions with staff and leadership at the institution were often met with apprehension. We did our best to allay the misconception that the research project would judge the value of the program itself rather than focus on sustainability.

Qualitative researchers must be particularly sensitive to ethical considerations (Patton, 2015). We passed the ethics clearance at the university level, but we would like to make it explicit that the purpose of our research

*Table 1.6* Summary of case studies

| Case study/ metaphors | Study participants | Data collection techniques |
| --- | --- | --- |
| Case study 1: technology as device | • Program coordinator<br>• Five instructors<br>• Researchers | • Semi-structured interviews<br>• Observations<br>• Document analysis<br>• Field notes |
| Case study 2: technology as system | • Program coordinator<br>• Curriculum review coordinator<br>• LMS project leader<br>• Four instructors<br>• Researchers | • Semi-structured interviews<br>• Document analysis<br>• Field notes |
| Case study 3: technology as application | • Program coordinator<br>• Deputy program coordinator<br>• Curriculum development coordinator<br>• Three instructors<br>• Researchers | • Semi-structured interviews<br>• Document analysis<br>• Field notes |

is not to make judgments but rather to make a move towards understanding how sustainability was enacted in blended language programs. As such, we seek to highlight the potential benefit of unpacking the factors that can help or hinder the sustainability of technology integration. Accordingly, we followed a suggestion to amend our original intent of the study. Rather than focussing on questions of pedagogical effectiveness, we began to focus more on the implementation of blended learning instead. Reassurances were also made regarding issues of anonymity and the removal of any details which could lead to the identification of the institution. After making the necessary amendments, a revised version of the proposal was resubmitted to the senior management, who approved the document and granted permission to conduct the research project.

In line with ethical practices, we sought to safeguard the anonymity of volunteer informants by omitting details that are of a private or sensitive nature (Bishop, 2012). We were especially sensitive to the concerns of those who may raise potentially controversial comments regarding the implementation of blended learning at the institution; accordingly, we use pseudonyms and remove any details which might lead to the identification of the respondents. Similarly, we seek to guard the anonymity the institution and its associated university. For this purpose, the institution is referred to as Royal College; in addition, participants were briefed to ensure they understood the purpose and objectives of the study, while consent forms were signed to indicate respondents' willingness to take part in the project in accordance with the ethical procedures of qualitative research (Patton, 2015).

In our analyses we sought to go beyond surface level (De Wever et al., 2006). To gain an overall idea of the interview data, for example, Cynthia listened to the interview recordings that she organised according to the category of participants. At this point, she developed detailed summaries of the interviews by extracting key content based on the interview questions. In a second cycle of analysis, the interview transcriptions and summaries were coded according to the four pillars of sustainable blended learning (Blin et al., 2016), and an initial list of categories and themes was developed. The process involved the systematic identification of patterns contained in the data to uncover pertinent themes which in turn served as units of analysis (Braun, Clarke, & Cooper, 2012). We then conducted a second round of analyses where we cross-checked an initial list of categories and themes with the interview transcriptions and summaries. As a result of this process, we regrouped certain categories into larger themes and sub-themes so that we could categorise the data. We repeated this process several times until we were satisfied that the most significant data were included, that all potential themes and sub-themes had been explored, and that the point of data saturation (Patton, 2015) had been reached. In the third stage, we mapped our emerging concepts into the sustainability framework (Blin et al., 2016). Also important, we made a note of data that could not be easily categorised into the existing pillars to determine if they could be recategorised, or whether the framework needed further extension through a new pillar(s). We then reanalysed the themes and subthemes to determine whether they could be further trimmed to reduce diffusion of concepts and remain directly relevant to sustainability and the long-term use of technology.

To maintain the validity and trustworthiness of the research process, several strategies were employed. First, data triangulation, or the verification of findings through multiple theoretical or methodological sources (Kress, 2011), was conducted. A key aspect of data trustworthiness was the role of Cynthia, who was part of the EAP academic team during the study. The experience provided insight into crucial aspects of the organisation, such as how the EAP program was run, how classes were conducted, and how the several types of technology were applied in class. Being a part of the day-to-day operations allowed Cynthia to gain insights as she grew to become a trusted member of the blended language program. Data from the collection such as interviews, field notes, and document analysis were cross-checked to uncover common themes and for data verification. In addition, member checks were conducted to ascertain the accuracy of the transcripts and interpretation of interview data (Koelsch, 2013) as well as confirm the validity of the findings. Each participant was given the opportunity to view and verify the interview transcripts and resulting analysis (member checking). Any discrepancies or item(s) that interviewees were not comfortable with were removed or modified accordingly.

## Summary of the chapter

The purpose of this chapter was to introduce the concept of sustainability through a brief overview of its history, its uses in environmental and development contexts, and a focus on the growing interest in the concept. Drawing on these aspects, sustainable technology integration is best understood as the long-term capacity of institutions to adapt their allocation of resources and practices to the ever-changing demands of contemporary education. Key to this definition of sustainability is that it prioritises a long-term vision or plan of change initiatives. Challenges that have impeded a sustained integration of educational technology include, for example, a lack of professional development that is needed for instructors to be able to use technology effectively, the eclectic nature of pedagogical decision making, and the development of technology-based 'innovations' by individual instructors that are not taken up by colleagues nor offered for widespread integration to the institute.

We chose to situate our conceptual framework with the ideas set out by Blin and colleagues (2016), who proposed four pillars of sustainability. Of these, the first stresses the need to take aspects of the environment and tools into account so that planning can identify key affordances that may bolster language learning. The next two pillars recognise the crucial role that instructional support plays in sustaining the integration of technology through both professional and community development. The fourth pillar holds organisational structure to inspection with a strong emphasis on the need for transparency, accountability, and dissemination of innovative practices. The model is to be interrogated with an argument-based approach, as advocated by Chapelle (2014), that was further developed by Gruba and colleagues (2016). Our chapter also included our approach to the study and detailed our methods, ethical considerations, and analytical processes. In the next chapter, we apply the concepts and an argument to interrogate the sustainability of technology using a device.

## References

Barlett, P. F., & Chase, G. W. (2013). *Sustainability in higher education: Stories and strategies for transformation.* MIT Press.

Bennett, S., Lockyer, L., & Agostinho, S. (2018). Towards sustainable technology-enhanced innovation in higher education: Advancing learning design by understanding and supporting teacher design practice. *British Journal of Educational Technology, 49*(6), 1014–1026.

Bishop, L. (2012). Using archived qualitative data for teaching: Practical and ethical considerations. *International Journal of Social Research Methodology, 15*(4), 341–350. doi:10.1080/13645579.2012.688335

Blin, F. (2016). Towards an "ecological" CALL theory: Theoretical perspectives and their instantiation in CALL research and practice. In F. Farr & L. Murray (Eds.), *The Routledge handbook of language learning and technology*. Routledge.

Blin, F., Jalkanen, J., & Taalas, P. (2016). Sustainable CALL development. In F. Farr & L. Murray (Eds.), *The Routledge handbook of language learning and technology* (pp. 223–238). Routledge.

Borowy, I. (2013). *Defining sustainable development for Our Common Future. A history of the World Commission on Environment and Development (Brundtland Commission)*. Taylor and Francis.

Bowen, G. A. (2009). Document analysis as a qualitative research method. *Qualitative Research Journal, 9*(2), 27–40. doi:10.3316/QRJ0902027

Bower, M., & Sturman, D. (2015). What are the educational affordances of wearable technologies? *Computers & Education, 88*, 343–353.

Braun, V., Clarke, V., & Cooper, H. (2012). Chapter 4: Thematic analysis. In H. Cooper, P. Camic, D. Long, A. Panter, D. Rindskopf, & K. Sher (Eds.), *APA handbook of research methods in psychology* (Vol. 2, pp. 57–71). American Psychological Association.

Brečko, B. N., Kampylis, P., & Punie, Y. (2014). *Mainstreaming ICT-enabled innovation in education and training in Europe: Policy actions for sustainability, scalability, and impact at system level*. Publications Office of the European Union. https://publications.jrc.ec.europa.eu/repository/handle/JRC83502

Brundtland, G. H. (1987). *Report of the World Commission on environment and development: 'Our Common Future'*. United Nations, available: http://www.un-documents.net/ocf-02.htm

Cerone, A. (2014). *Information technology and open source: Applications for education, innovation, and sustainability: SEFM 2012 Satellite Events, InSuEdu, MoKMaDS, and OpenCert, Thessaloniki, Greece, October 1–2, 2012: revised selected papers*. Springer.

Chapelle, C. A. (2009). The relationship between second language acquisition theory and computer-assisted language learning. *The Modern Language Journal, 93*, 741–753. doi:10.1111/j.1540-4781.2009.00970.x

Chapelle, C. A. (2014). Arguments for technology and language learning. Keynote presentation at *the EUROCALL 2014 Conference*. Groningen, the Netherlands. www.eurocall2014.nl/

Chapelle, C. A., Cotos, E., & Lee, J. (2015). Validity arguments for diagnostic assessment using automated writing evaluation. *Language Testing, 32*(3), 385–405. doi:10.1177/0265532214565386

Chapelle, C. A., Enright, M. K., & Jamieson, J. M. (2008). Test score interpretation and use. In M. K. Enright, C. A. Chapelle, & J. M. Jamieson (Eds.), *Building a validity argument for the Test of English as a Foreign Language* (pp. 1–25). Routledge.

Cuban, L. (2001). *Oversold and underused: Computers in the classroom*. Harvard University Press.

Davies, B., & West-Burnham, J. (Eds.). (2003). *Handbook of educational leadership and management*. Pearson Education.

## Situating sustainability

Denzin, N. K., & Lincoln, Y. S. (Eds.). (2003). *Collecting and interpreting qualitative materials* (2nd ed.). Sage.

De Wever, B., Schellens, T., Valcke, M., & Van Keer, H. (2006). Content analysis schemes to analyze transcripts of online asynchronous discussion groups: A review. *Computers & Education, 46*(1), 6–28. doi:10.1016/j.compedu.2005.04.005

Douglas Fir Group, T. (2016). A transdisciplinary framework for SLA in a multilingual world. *The Modern Language Journal, 100,* 19–47.

Eskildsen, S. W., & Theodórsdóttir, G. (2015). Constructing L2 learning spaces: Ways to achieve learning inside and outside the classroom. *Applied Linguistics, 38*(2), 143–165. doi:10.1093/applin/amv010

Fridley, D., & Rogers-Adkinson, D. (2015). Implementing a one-to-one technology initiative in higher education. *Administrative Issues Journal: Connecting Education, Practice, and Research, 5*(2), 38–50.

Gannaway, D., Hinton, T., Berry, B., & Moore, K. (2013). Cultivating change: Disseminating innovation in higher education teaching and learning. *Innovations in Education and Teaching International, 50*(4), 410–421.

Gimeno Sanz, A. M., Levy, M., Blin, F., & Barr, D. (2015). *WorldCALL: sustainability and computer-assisted language learning.* Bloomsbury.

Gleason, J. (2013). An interpretive argument for blended course design. *Foreign Language Annals, 46*(4), 588–609.

Golonka, E. M., Bowles, A. R., Frank, V. M., Richardson, D. L., & Freynik, S. (2014). Technologies for foreign language learning: A review of technology types and their effectiveness. *Computer Assisted Language Learning, 27*(1), 70–105. doi:10.1080/09588221.2012.700315

Gruba, P., Cardenas-Claros, M. S., Suvorov, R., & Rick, K. (2016). *Blended language program evaluation.* Palgrave Macmillan.

Gruba, P., & Hinkelman, D. (2012). *Blending technologies in second language classrooms.* Palgrave Macmillan.

Gunn, C. (2010). Sustainability factors for e-learning initiatives. *ALT-J: Research in Learning Technology, 18*(2), 89–103. doi:10.1080/09687769.2010.492848

Gunn, C. (2011). Sustaining eLearning innovations. In G. Williams, P. Statham, N. Brown, & B. Cleland (Eds.), *Changing demands, changing directions: Proceedings ascilite Hobart 2011* (pp. 509–519). www.ascilite.org.au/conferences/hobart11/procs/Gunn-full.pdf

Hall Giesinger, C., Adams Becker, S., Davis, A., and Shedd, L. (2016). *Scaling solutions to higher education's biggest challenges: An NMC Horizon Project strategic brief. Volume 3.2, October 2016.* The New Media Consortium.

Healey, D. (2016). Language learning and technology past, present and future. In F. Farr & L. Murray (Eds.), *The Routledge handbook of language learning and technology.* Routledge.

Hooey, C., Mason, A., & Triplett, J. (2017). Beyond greening: Challenges to adopting sustainability in institutions of higher education. *The Midwest Quarterly* (3), 280–291.

Hubbard, P. (2005). A review of subject characteristics in CALL research. *Computer Assisted Language Learning, 18*(5), 351–368.

Jones, D. P., & Johnstone, S. M. (2016). Responding to the challenge of sustainability. *Change: The Magazine of Higher Learning, 48*(4), 27–33.

Jones, P., Selby, D. D., & Sterling, S. R. (2010). *Sustainability education: Perspectives and practice across higher education*. Earthscan.

Kane, M. (2006). Validation. In R. Brennen (Ed.), *Educational measurement* (4th ed., pp. 17–64). Praeger.

Kennedy, C., & Levy, M. (2009). Sustainability and computer-assisted language learning: Factors for success in a context of change. *Computer Assisted Language Learning*, *22*(5), 445.

Koelsch, L. E. (2013). Reconceptualizing the member check interview. *International Journal of Qualitative Methods*, *12*(1), 168–179.

Kress, G. (2011). "Partnerships in research": Multimodality and ethnography. *Qualitative Research*, *11*(3), 239–260. doi:10.1177/1468794111399836

Lotherington, H. & Jenson, J. (2011). Teaching multimodal and digital literacy in L2 settings: New literacies, new basics, new pedagogies. *Annual Review of Applied Linguistics*, 31, 226–246. doi: 10.1017/S0267190511000110

Li, Y. (2015). Blended learning in English for tourism: A case study. In M. Li & Y. Zhao (Eds.), *Exploring learning & teaching in higher education* (pp. 331–345). Springer.

Littlejohn, A. (2003). Supporting sustainable e-learning. *ALT-J. Association for Learning Technology Journal*, *11*(3), 88.

Lynch, B. K. (2003). *Language assessment and programme evaluation*. Edinburgh University Press.

McDonald, P. (2014). Sustainability in CALL learning environments: A systemic functional grammar approach. *The EUROCALL Review*, *22*(2), 3–18.

McGill, T. J., Klobas, J. E., & Renzi, S. (2014). Critical success factors for the continuation of e-learning initiatives. *The Internet and Higher Education*, 22, 24–36.

Niederhauser, D. S., Howard, S. K., Voogt, J., Agyei, D. D., Laferriere, T., Tondeur, J., & Cox, M. J. (2018). Sustainability and scalability in educational technology initiatives: Research-informed practice. *Technology, Knowledge and Learning*, *23*(3), 507–523. doi:10.1007/s10758-018-9382-z

Nworie, J. (2014). Developing and sustaining instructional and technological innovations in teaching and learning. *Journal of Applied Learning Technology*, *4*(4), 5–14.

Owen, G. T. (2014). Qualitative methods in higher education policy analysis: Using interviews and document analysis. *Qualitative Report*, *19*(26), 1–19.

Patton, M. Q. (2015). *Qualitative research & evaluation methods: Integrating theory and practice* (4th ed.). SAGE Publications, Inc.

Pouezevara, S., Mekhael, S. W., & Darcy, N. (2014). Planning and evaluating ICT in education programs using the four dimensions of sustainability: A program evaluation from Egypt. *International Journal of Education and Development Using Information and Communication Technology*, *10*(2), 120–141.

Raji, M., & Zualkernan, I. (2016). A decision tool for selecting a sustainable learning technology intervention. *Journal of Educational Technology & Society*, *19*(3), 306–320.

Rick, K. (2016). A meso-level case study in Vietnam. In Gruba, P., Cardenas-Claros, M. S., Suvorov, R., & Rick, K. *Blended language program evaluation*. Palgrave Macmillan.

Robertson, I. (2008). Sustainable e-learning, activity theory and professional development. In Hello! Where are you in the landscape of educational technology?

Proceedings ascilite Melbourne 2008. http://www.ascilite.org.au/conferences/melbourne08/procs/robertson.pdf

Sayago, S. (2015). The construction of qualitative and quantitative data using discourse analysis as a research technique. *Quality & Quantity, 49*(2), 727–737. doi:10.1007/s11135-014-0020-0

Schalock, R. L., Verdugo, M., & Lee, T. (2016). A systematic approach to an organization's sustainability. *Evaluation and Program Planning, 56*, 56–63. doi:10.1016/j.evalprogplan.2016.03.005

Schulze, M., & Scholz, K. W. (2016). Complex adaptive systems in CALL research. In C. G. Caws & M. J. Hamel (Eds.), *Learner-computer interactions: New insights on CALL theories and applications* (pp. 65–88). John Benjamins.

Singh, G., & Hardaker, G. (2014). Barriers and enablers to adoption and diffusion of eLearning: A systematic review of the literature—A need for an integrative approach. *Education and Training, 56*(2), 105–121. doi:10.1108/ET-11-2012-0123

Spector, J. M. (2015). *Foundations of educational technology: Integrative approaches and interdisciplinary perspectives*. Routledge.

Stepanyan, K., Littlejohn, A., & Margaryan, A. (2013). Sustainable e-Learning: Toward a coherent body of knowledge. *Educational Technology & Society, 16*(2), 91–102.

Stern, D. M., & Willits, M. D. D. (2011). Social media killed the LMS: Re-imagining the traditional learning management system in the age of blogs and online social networks. In *Educating educators with social media* (pp. 347–373). Emerald Insight.

Tatum, B. D. (2013). The journey to green. In P. F. Barlett & G. W. Chase (Eds.), *Sustainability in higher education: Stories and strategies for transformation*. MIT Press.

Timmis, S. (2014). The dialectical potential of Cultural Historical Activity Theory for researching sustainable CSCL practices. *International Journal of Computer-Supported Collaborative Learning, 9*(1), 7–32. doi:10.1007/s11412-013-9178-z

Toh, Y. (2016). Leading sustainable pedagogical reform with technology for student-centred learning: A complexity perspective. *Journal of Educational Change, 17*(2), 145–169.

Waters, A. (2009). Managing innovation in English language education. *Language Teaching, 42*(4), 421–458. doi:10.1017/S026144480999005X

Yin, R. K. (2015). *Qualitative research from start to finish* (2nd ed.). Guilford Publications.

# 2 The sustainability of technology as a device in blended language programs

In the previous chapter, we set out our conceptual framework, explained our research design, and described our site of study and participants. In this chapter, we begin the first of our three case studies and interrogate the claim that technology integration based on a device is sustainable. We begin with a brief introduction of the device, a tablet computer (iPad). We situate the device at the site of study, and then follow the four stages that make up an argument-based approach: planning the argument, gathering the evidence, presenting the evidence, and appraising the claim. We conclude the chapter with a discussion of the sustainability of devices in blended language programs.

Following a federal government directive in 2012, each institute of higher education in the United Arab Emirates was provided with an iPad in the hopes that it would "provide a link between classroom and workplace skills and would increase test scores" (Johnston & Marsh, 2014, p. 51). As the researchers worked closely with teaching staff in their role of librarians, the researchers wrote about their experiences with the integration of the tablet computer in an EFL foundations course. They showed that instructors were overwhelmingly positive about the iPad because it fostered 'hands-on learning' approaches that engaged both instructors and students in several new ways. Because the use of the device caused such enthusiasm, the library staff "successfully embedded an information literacy curriculum" (Johnson & Marsh, 2104, p. 59) that in turn opened access to departmental meetings, materials design, and opportunities for collaboration that had previously not been possible.

For Ahmed and Nasser (2015), the iPad "has the capacity to create balanced and effective teaching and learning environments through highly engaging lessons, communication, and collaborative learning; the ability to foster creativity and learners' autonomy; and portability and quick and easy access to resources" (p. 755). Despite such enthusiasm for adoption, the researchers caution that "[t]echnology by itself does not guarantee effective

DOI: 10.4324/b22794-2

pedagogical practice and should not be used just for the sake of using it," but rather it "should be coupled with sound content knowledge and effective teaching methodologies" (Ahmed & Nasser, 2015, p. 763) to be both enjoyable and enable users to reach learning outcomes. With these studies and observations in mind, we turn our focus now to the use of iPads at our site of study.

## Investigating sustainable device use

Through a series of interviews with staff of Royal College, we came to understand that tablet computers were rolled out in three phases over two years. The first phase, a pilot study, began in 2010 when 50 students and 20 staff were provided with iPads. After undergoing initial training, the students and teachers were asked to integrate them into their classes and report on their experiences. The results of the pilot study demonstrated that there was an improvement in student results, a reduction in the use of paper materials, an increase in the storage, access, and sharing of course content, and improved communication between students and staff. Additionally, the pilot study reported that students liked the tablet computer because it was lightweight, portable, and enabled access to resources that could be used for research purposes.

As explained to us, the second phase of iPad rollout began in early 2011 when all staff were provided with tablet computers. Teacher training was widely supported, and included exposure to the broader set of technology resources available at Royal College. The purpose of the training was to encourage teachers to collaborate and develop materials, lesson plans, and assessments that made use of the tablet computers. Following a year of preparation, an iPad was given to each student who enrolled in the program from early 2012.

Prior to the introduction of tablet computers, Richard explained to us that all work was paper based. In practice, Richard noted, all lesson materials were printed for distribution and use. The paper textbook that was used at that time did not suit the full range of student proficiency levels. Earlier attempts to establish and integrate a learning management system (LMS) were thwarted in that the system was not set up properly, lacked consistency of presentation, and did not accord with the teachers' preferences for individual computers rather than a central online environment. The LMS was so cumbersome to use, Richard said, that most teachers did not bother to try it, anticipating certain failure.

Following years of service, Richard was appointed in 2015 as the program coordinator. In his new role, he began to advocate for the greater use of blended language learning approaches. According to Richard, he and his associate program coordinator, Ethan, transferred all EAP materials online using the Google suite of applications and shared these with the other teachers. Richard also renewed efforts to develop a web-based, open-source LMS (Moodle) to increase the use of self-access materials such as tests and lessons on vocabulary. With this facility, Richard began to advocate a 'flipped' approach whereby students could study content before it was covered in class to allow for more face-to-face discussions in the classroom. In addition to his development of the LMS, Richard created a website in the hopes that it would cultivate a greater sense of transparency for all staff and students in the program.

From its beginning, the EAP was designed to be a writing-focused program that enabled students to succeed in their studies at university level. The skills taught included essay planning, research, reading, and synthesizing academic articles as well as authoring an academic essay. To complement the program's traditional face-to-face activities, tablet computers were used for access to lesson materials and to carry out learning tasks. Each classroom was equipped with either a smart TV or projector that could be used to display material on the tablet computers. At the time of our study, the tablet computers were used to access Google Docs to facilitate collaborative writing processes in real time as part of the heavy emphasis on writing throughout the EAP program. Instructors were able to edit documents, give feedback, and monitor students' work without restrictions on time or place.

With regard to student access of lesson materials, the resources were made available in two formats in line with the preferences of each individual teacher. Some teachers preferred to use the evolving LMS platform as a central repository; others uploaded their class materials to Google Drive and then shared their work with their students. A central website contained information central to the entire EAP program, including subject outlines and assessment schedules, but was seen to be a static page with limited capabilities. Interestingly, although applications such as Good Reader, Keynote and ClickView were installed on each tablet computer, none of these were used by the teachers for any purpose during our study.

## Planning the argument

After reviewing the literature available on the EAP program and gaining ethics approval and entry to the site, we began to plan the argument and proceeded to map out the interpretive argument structure for a meso-level investigation of a blended language program (Table 2.1).

Based on Table 2.1, beginning with the target domain definition, the initial claim was laid out, which clearly specifies both the level and consideration of interest to the study (in this case the sustainability of technology use

*Table 2.1* Inferences, warrants, and assumptions of the argument

| Inferences | Warrants and assumptions (numbered after each warrant) |
| --- | --- |
| E. Ramification | An interrogation of sustainability as a device advances theory development and informs blended language learning approaches.<br>1. The findings are transferable to similar programs.<br>2. The findings are disseminated in an appropriate forum.<br>3. The research project interests the broader community. |
| D. Utilisation | The stakeholders make use of the findings to improve the program.<br>1. The findings resonate and are powerful enough to stimulate action.<br>2. The stakeholders take ownership of the findings.<br>3. The stakeholders can understand the findings. |
| C. Explanation | The findings are consistent with an understanding of the context of the study.<br>1. The intended use of tablet computers is understood by all stakeholders.<br>2. Sustainability, enacted through the purposeful application of tablet computers, is a goal of the institution.<br>3. Educational technology research is based on project criteria for course, professional, or theoretical development. |
| B. Evaluation | The analysis identifies the institutional stance towards sustainability as a device in blended learning.<br>1. The analysis is accurate, robust, and trustworthy.<br>2. The analytical processes are conducted in ways that are appropriate and ethical to the field.<br>3. Discourse analysis can identify themes regarding the sustainability of tablet computers.<br>4. The use of tablet computers in the EAP program represents the area to be evaluated. |
| A. Domain definition | The use of a device or tablet computer is sustainable in the EAP program.<br>1. Policies at Royal College indicate reasons for the use of educational technologies and how such use can be sustained.<br>2. Language learning is an institutional concern.<br>3. Blended learning is a goal in the use of educational technologies.<br>4. Educational technologies are a matter of concern for all stakeholders. |

Source: Adapted from Gruba et al. (2016)

conducted at the meso level). In other words, the target domain definition provides the context of the case study in terms of what is being investigated, at what level, and through which consideration. This was followed by laying out the underlying warrants and assumptions behind the claim. This same process of laying out the claim for each inference (evaluation, explanation, utilisation, and ramification), together with the corresponding warrants and assumptions, was repeated until the interpretive argument structure was complete.

## Gathering the evidence

Informed by the framework of Blin, Jalkanen, and Taalas (2016), data from reflective journal entries, Cynthia's field notes, and other teachers' class observations and experiences, interviews with the subject leader and EAP teachers as well as informal conversations with students were analysed. The findings of our study of the use of tablet computers rely on the four pillars of sustainable blended learning (Blin et al., 2016).

### *Pillar 1: environments and tools for learning*

In the first pillar, Blin et al. (2016) argue that the environments and tools for learning used by a blended language program should be purposeful and tailored to the needs of students, teachers, learning objectives, and activities. In terms of learning environments, based on analysis of curriculum documents and teachers' lesson plans, the EAP program's focus was on collaborative and individual writing. Thus, the use of tablet computers to deliver the course content influenced the kind of learning environment created.

Before going to work at Royal College, Cynthia anticipated some resistance to technology, especially from staff who had been teaching prior to the introduction of tablet computers into the EAP program. Through her first round of observations with all full-time teachers, she noted the range of interpretations when it came to blended learning and each teacher's implementation of such an approach based on their understanding and teaching philosophies. These factors influenced the learning environment teachers created for their respective classes. For example, Patricia prioritised a keen understanding of the lesson content as well as conducting oral class discussions. Keeping technology use at a minimum, she spent more time teaching face to face, using tablet computers only to complete online tasks. She also went through the answers with the whole class, asking each student in turn to provide their answers. Other teachers, like Alice and Kristen, had a more equal balance of online and face-to-face elements. The first half of class was typically spent on face-to-face lesson delivery and providing clear, step-by-step instructions on class activities. The remainder of the time was spent on teacher consultations with each group while other groups worked on online collaborative writing tasks using Google Docs. On the other hand, Karla minimised teacher talk time, relying heavily on Google Docs for online collaborative work. As students were working on live documents, Karla also gave feedback and monitored students' work from the online interface.

Another aspect of the learning environment relates to students' classroom experiences. Through observations of her own and other teachers' classes, what Cynthia found most striking was how isolating and passive a writing class could be when using a tablet computer to facilitate the writing process. She noted how most students were on their tablet computers and class interaction was minimal. Even when group members worked collaboratively on the same essay document in Google Docs, Cynthia noted that the approach did not encourage discussion because group members tended to work individually on an allocated section of the collaborative essay task. Excerpts from an interview with Rachel concur:

> Well, I don't like it that it is so writing based. I mean I try to get them to have confidence in speaking as I think that confidence boosts their writing and their reading as well. And I think just the process of discussing something and then writing is more stimulating for them . . . just more communicative. To me that's more authentic.
> (Rachel, Int. 01, Lines 53–54)

For some of the teachers, active student discussions and interactions were associated with 'more authentic' learning experiences, and the use of tablet computers did not seem to encourage such experiences.

The final aspect with regard to learning environments is how the use of the tablet computer affected classroom management. An interview with the program coordinator (Richard) revealed that too many platforms were used (applications, LMS, Google Sites, and Google Docs/ Drive), resulting in a lack of integration and a feeling of being overwhelmed. Interviews with teachers confirmed this, with one teacher commenting that

> on the tablet computer switching back and forth from Google Sites to LMS to other documents is frustrating as I need to get out of a website and then into LMS . . . easier if all the materials were centralized.
> (Rachel, Int. 01, Lines 41,46)

Field notes and observation data also show that the lack of multi-window functionality in the present tablet computer (2017) made it difficult for students to carry out essay writing tasks that required the use of other documents such as research articles, lesson materials, or rubrics. The lack of a multi-screen functionality has led to the use of additional devices where both teachers and students have been observed using additional laptops and even mobile phones to carry out class activities.

A related and key factor of learning environments is the tools used for learning. In the case of the EAP program, tablet computers are the primary tool specifically for its perceived efficacy as a teaching tool. The full rollout of tablet computers at Royal College was particularly significant given the college's heavy investment in them as the main technological tool used in the classroom. Every student received a tablet computer during their orientation which they were able to keep even after they completed their studies at the institution. Similarly, teaching staff also received a tablet computer during staff induction sessions which they were to use for teaching purposes. However, should they leave the institution they were required to return the device. Through my own experiences, observations, interviews with the subject leader and other teachers as well as informal conversations with students, it was confirmed that the tablet computer was not useful as a teaching tool. Data from interviews, field notes, and observations revealed that the tablet computer fell short in terms of hardware and software limitations. Regarding hardware, limitations included the small screen size, the touch-screen feature, and the lack of a physical keyboard; for software, there were incompatabilites with other operating systems, networking lag, and an absence of installed preferred applications.

Besides reading, writing on a tablet computer was also problematic and highlights its shortcomings for use as an educational device. In her field notes, Cynthia recorded frustration as the touch-screen feature made editing tasks such as highlighting, copying, and rearranging words, sentences, and paragraphs quite difficult. The lack of a keyboard also affected writing tasks in that tapping on the screen of a tablet computer was not as efficient as typing on a physical keyboard. Students in informal chats expressed a preference for a physical keyboard to make activities much easier and more enjoyable. Unsurprisingly, in her teaching Cynthia also observed that many students added an external keyboard to their tablet computers or simply brought in their own laptop computer. As shown in the work of Green, Naidoo, Olminkhof, and Dyson (2016), the tablet computer was used primarily for the consumption of content (e.g., following lessons, accessing course materials, going through recommended readings) rather than the creation of content (e.g., writing, doing audio-visual recordings).

Significantly, the iPad is incompatible with Android computers and systems. Interviews with teachers revealed that some were using Android computers, which required them to switch between devices and made working from home difficult. For example, after editing their documents on their Android computer and then opening them on the tablet computer, documents did not always display correctly, and the layout of text was affected. Students also reported similar experiences when switching between devices, with many stating their preference for the Android operating system. For such students, conflicts that arose as they tried to bridge the two operating systems weakened an initial resolve to work on tablet computers.

From the discussion of Pillar 1 findings, it is unsurprising that teachers strongly recommended that laptops be adopted or that students be required to bring their own devices. The tablet computers were simply not working well, as Richard suggests:

> The tablet computer is not the best device for a blended program as it is not designed as an educational tool but more for personal leisure and entertainment as it has some fairly obvious limitations.
> (Richard, Int. 01, Line 15)

### *Pillar 2: pedagogical and professional development*

The second pillar, on pedagogical and professional development, acknowledges teachers' roles as change agents of new teaching initiatives. As such, the sustainability of blended learning rests on their ability to continuously adapt their teaching practices in line with changing classroom environments. Interview data show that teachers do recognise the importance of technology in teaching, especially the role that it plays in online collaborative writing, which is central to the EAP curriculum. However, it was found that teachers displayed varying degrees of technology resistance due to "insecurity, lack of confidence in trying to manipulate a new kind of skills" (Kristen, Int. 01, Line 40). The skill areas which teachers felt needed further development included teaching methodology, materials development in an online format, and exploring programs/tools which can facilitate class activities. The following interview response reflects this third concern:

> So, for example, if you were not aware that certain programs exist . . . say you're doing a language quiz where you want them to choose certain answers and get some feedback (a) you've got to know that there are programs that can do that, (b) you've got to have the time to set it up the first place.
> (Alice, Int. 01, Line 18)

In general, teachers expressed the need for continuous and targeted professional development and training on the pedagogical reasoning and application of tablet computers in relation to EAP course content. At the time of the study, the focus of teacher professional development had been more on the technical aspects of setting up and using tablet computers as well as exposure to educational applications that teachers could use in the classroom. Much less attention had been given to demonstrations featuring how teachers could design lessons and tasks to create lessons that 'work' in the online format. Similar conclusions on the lack of training on the pedagogical applications of technology use have been reported in the literature (Kennedy & Levy, 2009).

In terms of interactions among the pillars, the lack of initial training created conflict with environments. In this context, due to the lack of targeted training on how to integrate tablet computers in the classroom, this affected teachers' motivation to use such devices because they were not fully informed on its use and the design of lessons incorporating technology. In other words, deficiencies in the pedagogical and professional development pillar negatively affected the resulting environments and tools for learning.

## *Pillar 3: community and knowledge building*

The third pillar underscores the need for collaboration and for teachers to continuously adapt their teaching views and practices, in line with the corresponding tools and environments for learning. Thus, Pillar 3 can have a direct effect on Pillar 1. Interview data revealed the need for greater internal and external collaborations to promote sustained blended learning practices. For internal collaboration, teachers expressed the need for EAP teachers to work together and share their expertise. For external collaboration, this involves an awareness of what teachers are doing in other foundation program subjects such as biology, mathematics, and media communications. Such an awareness can better inform teachers on how the knowledge students gain from EAP can support non-EAP subjects. Such collaboration can facilitate knowledge building through a greater subject alignment to benefit both teachers and students. For teachers, such initiatives may lead to greater awareness on selecting more relevant class materials, as Karla suggests:

> I'd like to use a lot more material from biology, sciences, commerce, or finance, as an authentic way of understanding the information they're reading. I'm a fan of using authentic material, authentic texts and if we're making it up then we're not preparing them for realistic application of those skills. In that sense, we need to know what everybody else is doing so that we can relate to them and prepare students to be able to

do that in real time, in those subjects and then later on be comfortable enough to perform those functions at university.

(Karla, Int. 01, Lines 55–60)

Another aspect of sustainability under this pillar is the need for community and knowledge-building practices to adapt and evolve according to the changing needs of teachers, students, and the EAP program itself. The importance of teachers to come together and work on continuous course refinement was highlighted in teacher interviews. Each teacher expressed a general satisfaction with the EAP curriculum but felt that constant revisions were needed. Teachers were working individually on each of these resources to simplify tasks for lower-level students, for example, as well as to create extension activities for higher-level classes, but there was little central coordination.

Although these initiatives have the potential to improve the sustainability of teaching resources, the interaction of organisational structures created conflict in the development of a community of practice. The lack of clear organisational structures (Pillar 3) in establishing formalised procedures for documenting modifications in teaching resources diminished the scalability aspect of sustainability. In this regard, adaptations were not disseminated to the rest of the EAP main program teachers, and the resulting breakdown in community and knowledge-building practices led to lost opportunities for refining curriculum materials to be used for subsequent iterations of the course.

### *Pillar 4: organisational structures*

The fourth pillar relates to how change should be implemented across all levels in relation to broader institutional objectives and being able to adjust to possible unexpected outcomes in the process. To foster multi-level stakeholder involvement to support change initiatives, the institution needs to establish a sharp vision of technology integration and the roles of stakeholders at various levels. By establishing clarity in organisational structures, stakeholders can be held accountable for aligning their practices to broader institutional objectives. Analysis of interview data reaches similar conclusions where the need for a top-down approach to implementing blended learning initiatives was proposed. An excerpt from an interview with a teacher, Kristen, illustrates this point:

So that means as an organization higher up—they do have a vision. I mean they know what kind of approach they're using and then that message needs to be communicated to the teachers and the students.

(Kristen, Int. 01, Lines 22–23)

During our research, it became apparent that organisational structures were fractured because of a lack of a clear blended-learning policy that could streamline the use of technology throughout all programs of Royal College. The lack of policy was confirmed through interviews with the program coordinator and teachers, as well as a document analysis of the college portal and website. Interviews with teachers revealed that there was strong encouragement from the upper management to use technology and tablet computers for teaching. As Richard observed, teachers may not have been fully aware of the stated vision of Royal College to advance teaching practices using technology. The lack of a formal policy on technology use diminished a sense of ownership and any uptake of teaching initiatives.

In his roles as both a teacher and program coordinator, Richard was able to view technology integrations from a range of perspectives. Ideally, the ability to implement technology change initiatives from multiple perspectives could promote greater alignment in organisational structures as upper management decisions could respond to micro-level insights. In the case of tablet computers, however, a range of emerging issues that emanated from the classroom were not surfaced at the macro level; accordingly, they lost motivation to continue to use the device and thus fulfil the institution's broader technology integration goals. Though possible, the lack communication at the meso level resulted in missed opportunities to adjust iPad use in response to either macro-level directives or micro-level concerns.

## Appraising the argument

With the completion of the first three stages of the argument-based approach, we can now interrogate the claim that the use of tablet computers is sustainable within the blended approaches to language learning at Royal College. To start, the domain definition inference is founded on the warrant that the integration of tablet computers can be facilitated and supported over the long-term and demonstrate the long-term capacity of socio-cultural and technical systems to exist in ever-evolving educational spaces. Our review of the literature showed that many educational institutions were integrating the use of tablet computers during the period 2010–2018; here, then, decisions to adopt the iPad throughout the Royal College university pathways program was based on several sources. For the domain inference, the evidence is strong and supports the move to the next inference of the argument. Thus, we were assured that data collection at the site would not be futile.

The inference of evaluation considers the appropriateness of data collection and analysis and seeks to identify the stance of the program towards the sustainable the use of the iPad. Through both document analysis and the ethnography, we were able to gather data that revealed themes that accord with the work of Blin and colleagues (2016). The inference of evaluation has been met and is strong, thus the argument can proceed.

The explanation inference is based on the warrant that the findings are consistent with an understanding of the context of the evaluation. The key assumption for this inference is that sustainability, enacted through reuse and repurposing, is a goal of the institution. Considering our findings, however, such assumptions are not backed by the evidence: that is, despite years of tablet computer usage, integration of the device was not supported by robust evidence. On the contrary, we found that issues of use at the meso level (lack of ongoing training, for example) as well at the micro level (difficulties in creating content, for example) belied the reduced support by the institution at the macro level. In short, as challenges arose in integration at lower levels, the lack of policy and encouragement by the college leadership eventually led to the withdrawal of the tablet computer across the pathways program. At this point, the argument cannot proceed, and it reveals factors that preclude any further movement in the interpretative argument towards the inferences of utilisation and ramification.

To conclude, we have seen that the claim 'the use of tablet computers is sustainable in the blended language program' is weak; that is, an idea that a device enhances sustainable practices is rebutted as it has not been fully met at this time. In line with the effort by Golonka, Bowles, Frank, Richardson, and Freynik (2014) to evaluate the strength of claims, any suggestion that key stakeholders, primarily teachers, make use of devices in ways that enhance sustainability in blended learning would be at best 'moderate'. That is, although the first two inferences of domain definition and evaluation were met, neither explanation nor utilisation inferences could be fully supported. Regarding the inference of explanation, for example, matters of sustainable practices at the case study institution appeared to be at aspirational stages and were yet to be fully developed. For utilisation, this limited case study cannot assert that institutional stakeholders will incorporate any of the findings in their future work.

As demonstrated by the appraisal, an argument for the sustainable use of the tablet computer could not progress, as evidence revealed how assumptions pertaining to an explanation broke down. Specifically, difficulties that appeared at lower levels of the institution were not sufficiently addressed by leadership, for example. In their defence, however, it possible that upper college administration were not made aware of issues being experienced by instructors and students; on a global level, too, the novelty of tablet computers for classroom usage had begun to wane (Porter, Graham, Bodily, & Sandberg, 2016). If anything, trends began to emerge during this period to encourage staff and students to 'bring your own device' (BYOD) and thus reduce the pressure on institutions to provide technical support, funding, and training, while at the same time increasing sustainable use of technology (Engin & Donanci, 2015).

## Summary of the chapter

Not surprisingly, our case study demonstrated that the use of tablet computers in this blended learning program was not sustainable. We support such a conclusion by showing that claims in the interpretive argument structure were not supported. In summary, we found that the tablet computers did not meet the pillars of sustainability for environments and tools for learning, pedagogical and professional development, community and knowledge building, or organisational structures (Blin et al., 2016). The device was not seen as fit for purpose for students because it was not useful as a tool for extensive academic writing; teachers withdrew their support of the device out of frustration with its limitations; program leadership began to develop a larger, central system that did not encourage tablet computer use; macro-level institutional leadership did not provide ongoing support including professional development opportunities and strong policies.

In the next chapter, we interrogate the sustainability of 'technology as a system' that merges a complicated network of inter-related components into a unified whole (Banathy & Jenlink, 2004; Ison, 2008). Therefore, the focal technology to be investigated will shift to the LMS utilised in the college, where a similar approach will be undertaken through a qualitative case study structured through the interpretive argument framework.

## References

Ahmed, K., & Nasser, O. (2015). Incorporating iPad technology: Creating more effective language classrooms. *TESOL Journal*, *6*, 751–765. doi:10.1002/tesj.192

Banathy, B. H., & Jenlink, P. M. (2004). Systems inquiry and its application in education. In D. H. Jonassen (Ed.), *Handbook of research on educational communications and technology* (2nd ed., pp. 37–57). Lawrence Erlbaum.

Blin, F., Jalkanen, J., & Taalas, P. (2016). Sustainable CALL development. In F. Farr & L. Murray (Eds.), *The Routledge handbook of language learning and technology* (pp. 223–238). Routledge.

Engin, M., & Donanci, S. (2015). Dialogic teaching and tablet devices in the EAP classroom. *Computers & Education*, *88*, 268–279. doi:10.1016/j.compedu.2015.06.005

Golonka, E. M., Bowles, A. R., Frank, V. M., Richardson, D. L., & Freynik, S. (2014). Technologies for foreign language learning: A review of technology types and their effectiveness. *Computer Assisted Language Learning*, *27*(1), 70–105.

Green, D., Naidoo, E., Olminkhof, C., & Dyson, L. E. (2016). Tablets@university: The ownership and use of tablet devices by students. *Australasian Journal of Educational Technology*, *32*(3), 50–64.

Gruba, P., Cardenas-Claros, M. S., Suvorov, R., Rick, K. (2016). *Blended language program evaluation*. Palgrave Macmillan.

Ison, R. (2008). Systems thinking and practice for action research. In P. Reason & H. Bradbury (Eds.), *The SAGE handbook of action research: Participative inquiry and practice* (pp. 139–158). Sage.

Johnston, N., & Marsh, S. (2014). Using iBooks and iPad apps to embed information literacy into an EFL foundations course. *New Library World, 115*(1/2), 51–60. doi:10.1108/NLW-09-2013-0071

Kennedy, C., & Levy, M. (2009). Sustainability and computer-assisted language learning: Factors for success in a context of change. *Computer Assisted Language Learning, 22*(5), 445.

Porter, W. W., Graham, C. R., Bodily, R. G., & Sandberg, D. S. (2016). A qualitative analysis of institutional drivers and barriers to blended learning adoption in higher education. *The Internet and Higher Education, 28*, 17–27.

# 3 The sustainability of a system in blended language programs

In the previous chapter, we saw how the sustainable use of tablet computers may not have rested solely on the device itself but may have been caused by factors such as a lack of teacher professional development or a deep resistance to technology. The notion of a sum being greater than its parts (Ison, 2008), as such, suggests the need for a broader view of technology as a complex interaction of components working together as a unified whole (Banathy & Jenlink, 2004). Accordingly, this chapter departs from a device-focused to a systems-focused view of technology through a study of the institutional proprietary learning management system (LMS) to investigate a single claim: the LMS is a key component of blended language learning sustainability. Going beyond the technical aspects involved when teachers work with the LMS as a system, the case study in this chapter seeks to uncover the complexities involved when groups of teachers collaborate through the process of initial planning, materials design, and the subsequent translation of the designed learning materials into the LMS format.

## Understanding systems

Before moving further, it is necessary to have a better understanding of what is meant by a system. In general, 'system' refers to a regular set of factors/ elements that have been designed to structure a series of actions (Mele, Pels, & Polese, 2010). In more conceptual terms, there has been no consensus on what 'system' means (Patton, 2011) as it has been defined in a variety of ways. For our purposes, we follow Ison (2008) who highlights the Greek origins of the term which mean 'to place together' (p. 142) to emphasise the nature of interactions that may occur amongst a range of various elements. With reference to language education, the term has been used to reference structured institutional policies (Demirkan, 2010), a structured set of principles that underpin approaches to blended learning (Hinkelman, 2018), or a set of forms or executable tasks designed to enhance teaching and learning

DOI: 10.4324/b22794-3

(Kubanyiova & Crookes, 2016). As we can see, any 'system' can become extraordinarily complex; to inform research in the area, systems theory or 'the science of complexity' was developed in the 1950s through the work of a multi-disciplinary group which sought to provide insights into the universality of world experiences (Banathy & Jenlink, 2004).

Over time, theories of 'systems thinking' evolved to provide in-depth understanding of a system's components, the interactions among those components, and the interventions necessary to produce more positive outcomes (Arnold & Wade, 2015). It is interesting to note that for such an important concept, there has been no consensus on the exact meaning of systems thinking, with the definition having undergone various interpretations throughout the literature (Arnold & Wade, 2015). Through an analysis of the various systems thinking definitions put forward by different researchers, they concluded that none of the proposed definitions covered aspects of purpose, components, and the inter-relationships between those components that they saw to be essential for a holistic definition of systems thinking (Arnold & Wade, 2015). To offset existing limitations, Arnold and Wade (2015) applied the principles of systems thinking into systems thinking itself to highlight the purpose, components, and interactions between those components:

> Systems thinking is a set of synergistic analytic skills used to improve the capability of identifying and understanding systems, predicting their behaviours, and devising modifications to them in order to produce desired effects. These skills work together as a system.
> (Arnold & Wade, 2015, p. 675)

Although this definition draws on Ison (2008), it adds the essential element of *purpose* into systems thinking. As such, the strength of systems thinking lies in its capacity to provide explanatory and predictive power with regard to understanding complex situations or behaviour (Arnold & Wade, 2015; Patton, 2011). Relating to innovation and developmental research studies, Patton (2011) postulates that the notion of complexity is characterised by non-linearity, emergence, dynamical systems, adaptiveness, uncertainty, and coevolution. Methodologies employing system dynamics involve a cyclical and iterative process of 'feedback loops' as a catalyst for further adjustments (Patton, 2011, p. 139). Applying a systems thinking approach enables researchers to offer valuable insights on how decisions and initiatives implemented on a broader organisational level are in turn being interpreted, translated, and responded to by various stakeholders (Patton, 2011).

In relation to systems thinking are systems approaches which combine systemic and systematic thinking (Ison, 2008). While both modes of thinking have a deep appreciation of the broader context in which a phenomenon occurs, Ison (2008) contends that the main distinction lies in the type of interactions occurring among the different components. For systemic thinking, interactions between components are more dynamic and constitute the knowledge of cycles, counterintuitive effects, and unintended consequences, whereas for systematic thinking, the interactions are viewed in a more methodical, stepwise fashion (Ison, 2008).

Thus far, we have looked at the definition of systems and systems thinking and seen how, for systems thinking, a phenomenon must be understood in terms of its purpose, components, and the interactions between components. In the same way, systems thinking can also be applied to technology, observing that complex adaptive systems are made up of different components with complex interactions all working synergistically to fulfil the system's intended objectives (Schulze & Scholz, 2016). Accordingly, Bax (2011) cautions against attributing the success or failure of 'normalising' technology in educational settings based on the dichotomy between the device used (for example, tablet computers) and the people using it (for example, teachers). Bax argues that holding such a dichotomous view of technology integration suggests that such initiatives are somehow independent of a host of larger extenuating factors.

Relating to the earlier discussion of systems thinking, the issues surrounding technology integration are far more complex and often require a continuous cycle of improvements based on the feedback received. In the specific context of blended language learning, Bax (2011) cautions against the tendency for oversimplification, arguing for a broader view of the various socio-cultural factors at play when teachers make use of technology. Similar views are held by Gruba and Hinkelman (2012), who call for a much wider conceptualisation of technology to go beyond limited 'device-only' views.

Bringing together the concepts of systems and systems thinking in the literature and how these concepts relate to technology, a case can now be built that the LMS can exemplify a broader view of technology as a system, since it is made up of various interacting components, which ideally contribute to the singular purpose of enhancing pedagogy. Through this lens, the LMS is regarded in this case study as a dynamic, collaborative, and adaptive system (Schulze & Scholz, 2016) that involves teachers working together to develop online materials and lessons, to maintain the sustainability of blended learning through capacity building initiatives. Such initiatives involve, for example, providing the necessary professional development training so that teachers themselves will be able to develop online materials using the institutional LMS.

The LMS can be regarded as a typical, if not the most used, technological system at many institutions of higher learning (Stern & Willits, 2011). A common view of an LMS is a platform from which an educational program can host its course content (e.g., syllabi, lessons, resources, lesson activities) as well as handle administrative tasks such as grading and assignment submissions (Zanjani, Edwards, Nykvist, & Geva, 2017). However, for Stern and Willits (2011), the focus should ideally go beyond the technical aspects of the LMS and move towards questioning the rationale behind the purpose and organisation of the LMS in terms of achieving teaching and learning outcomes. In other words, more than what the LMS is capable of, what needs particular emphasis is what pedagogical value the LMS can bring to both students and teachers. What needs to be questioned is not merely the potential affordances of the LMS but the educational purposes that drive the use of the LMS in the first place (Hinkelman, 2018). Another related issue in terms of the LMS as a system is its organisational structure, which can be regarded as hierarchical as opposed to a bottom-up system (Stern & Willits, 2011, p. 356).

In the context of this study, the LMS's hierarchical system means that teachers are not involved in aspects such as the LMS interface design, which is typically done by the ITS (information technology services) of an institution. Typically, there is not much room for teachers to be creative in the look and feel of a site as they need to work within the constraints of the LMS. According to my interview data, teachers not only had to follow the organisation of the page, but they also had to follow a laborious set of procedures to upload materials, prompting many to conclude that the LMS is not particularly user friendly.

The key to the success of the curriculum review initiative was the implementation of the LMS Development Project. More specifically, the project enabled the EAP department to address key issues, including the lack of IT skills, insufficient IT, media and e-learning support, and the absence of qualified instructional designers, which negatively affected sustainability. Thus, the onus fell on teachers, who were tasked to become content creators and online-material designers. Through the LMS Development Project, selected EAP academic staff would need to be equipped with the training and skills to transfer online content from an existing platform, or design and develop new online content for the LMS used by the EAP program.

Teachers needed to learn to convert the paper-based tasks into online document that, in turn, would be shared. By working with the same content in a more dynamic format, the teachers hoped that groups of students would eventually be able to engage in more collaborative work using live documents. Teachers hoped that they would also be able to track class progress more efficiently as student work could be monitored in real time. No longer, the teachers hoped, would they need to move around the classroom to monitor individual or group work; it could be done electronically. In addition, teachers were hoping to be able to collaborate with students in real time by typing comments and providing feedback throughout live sessions.

## Planning the argument

Let us now shift our focus to planning the argument. Following preliminary discussions with program leaders, we built a structure (Table 3.1) to evaluate technology as a system and its relation to blended learning sustainability.

As shown in Table 3.1, beginning with the target domain definition, the central claim is laid out that the LMS provides an ideal system through which capacity building initiatives help to promote blended language learning sustainability. This claim builds on the previous case study in Chapter 4 which found that a device view of technology was not sustainable and therefore would need to be expanded. The underlying assumptions of this claim were that the use of the LMS would improve security,

*Table 3.1* Inferences, warrants, and assumptions in the argument

| Inferences | Warrants and assumptions (numbered after each warrant) |
|---|---|
| **E. Ramification** | An investigation of sustainability as a system advances theory development and improves approaches to research blended language learning. |
| | 1. The findings are transferable to similar programs. |
| | 2. The findings are disseminated in an appropriate forum. |
| | 3. The research project interests the broader community. |
| **D. Utilisation** | An understanding of sustainability as a system encourages stakeholders to make use of the findings to improve the program. |
| | 1. The findings resonate and are powerful enough to stimulate action. |
| | 2. The stakeholders take ownership of the findings. |
| | 3. The stakeholders can understand the findings. |
| | 4. The findings can be used to identify gaps in the blended learning system to improve sustainability. |
| **C. Explanation** | The findings are consistent with an understanding of the context of the investigation. |
| | 1. The intended use of the LMS is understood by all stakeholders. |
| | 2. Sustainability, enacted through the capacity building of teachers, is a goal of the organisation. |
| | 3. Educational technology research is based on project criteria for course, professional, or theoretical development. |

(*Continued*)

Table 3.1 (Continued)

| Inferences | Warrants and assumptions (numbered after each warrant) |
|---|---|
| **B. Evaluation** | The analysis identifies key elements of the program that influence the sustainability of technology as a system in blended learning.<br>1. The analysis is accurate, robust, and trustworthy.<br>2. The analytical processes are transparent, appropriate, and ethical.<br>3. Qualitative analysis can identify themes regarding sustainability as a system.<br>4. The use of the LMS in an EAP program represents the area to be evaluated. |
| **A. Domain definition** | The LMS provides an ideal environment for blended language learning in ways that enhance pedagogy, mutual support, professional development, and sustainability.<br>1. The central interactive environment LMS improves pedagogy and teamwork.<br>2. LMS materials design improves teacher motivation by providing opportunities for collaboration and upskilling.<br>3. Teachers can develop skills for online materials development easily.<br>4. The use of an LMS provides a secure and coherent educational environment for student interaction, materials deposit, and record keeping. |

Source: Adapted from Gruba, Cardenas-Claros, Suvorov, & Rick (2016)

enhance teacher motivation, and enable teachers to easily develop skills in online materials development. Building from the domain inference, is evaluation, which is dependent on an accurate and thorough analysis of the data according to the study context. The interpretive argument then moves on to the remainder of the inferences, culminating in ramification, which refers to the potential utility and transferability of the study outcomes into other contexts.

## Gathering the evidence

With the development of the interpretive argument structure which maps out the investigation's inferential claims together with the corresponding warrants and assumptions, the next stage of the investigation involved gathering the evidence either to support or refute the claims made at each stage of the investigation. To this end, the section that follows provides further details on the methodology, participants, and data collection techniques employed in this case study. With an understanding of the project's background and

*A system in blended language programs* 43

*Table 3.2* Summary of data collection techniques

| Level | Target | Duration/ frequency | Method | Area of focus/pillar focus (Blin et al., 2016) |
|---|---|---|---|---|
| Meso | Subject leader of the EAP program | Approx. 30–45 mins./ two times at the beginning and end of course | Semi-structured interview | Development and implementation of LMS as capacity building initiative |
|  | Curriculum Review Project Coordinator | Approx. 30 mins./one time | Semi-structured interview | Development and implementation of the Curriculum Review Project and how this relates to LMS projects |
| Micro | 3 EAP teachers | Approx. 30–45 mins/ one time | Semi-structured interviews | • The use of the LMS as a technological tool (Pillars 2 & 4)<br>• Affordances and limitations of materials development through LMS<br>• How blended learning was implemented through LMS materials/ lessons in the classroom<br>• Factors influencing sustainability of LMS at meso level (Pillars 1, 2, & 3) |

cycles, a summary of the data collection techniques employed in this study is shown in Table 3.2.

As shown in Table 3.2, the data collection techniques employed in this case study can be divided into the meso and micro levels. For the meso level, interviews with program administrators were conducted to provide an administrative perspective regarding the LMS capacity building initiative in relation to the broader Curriculum Review Project. As for micro-level data, three teachers from the Intensive program were interviewed. The focus of the interviews was on the use of the LMS and covered several aspects such as pedagogical applications, its impact on materials development work, and the factors influencing sustainability at the micro level.

## Presenting the argument

In this second case study, we examined claims regarding technology as a system and provided two different perspectives on how materials development in the LMS were conducted in the EAP department at Royal College.

Accordingly, the findings section is divided into two broad sections, the first one concerned with the LMS Migration Project and Cynthia's experiences as a committee member. Here, the main data sources are more autoethnographic in nature and based primarily on her field notes.

The second part of our presentation focuses on the LMS Capacity Building Project and incorporates data of a more ethnographic orientation through interviews and document analysis. In line with our study of tablet computers, the findings are discussed in relation to the pillars of sustainable blended learning proposed by Blin et al. (2016). To reiterate, they are: (1) environments and tools for learning, (2) pedagogical and professional development, (3) community and knowledge building, and (4) organisational structures.

In contrast to the first LMS project, a second project to do with LMS capacity building required teachers to develop materials. Unfortunately, they had no foundation of existing materials from which to build upon. Compared to the first LMS Migration Project, the process of 'capacity building' was quite daunting for some teachers, especially those who had restricted time. For some teachers, however, this second project did have the appeal of starting fresh without influence from previous materials that allowed for creativity. Both types of teachers, however, soon realised that materials development was a time-consuming process and this second project soon lost widespread support. Our analysis of the data reveals a range of issues and themes that emerged in this attempt to use the LMS as a sustainable technology in the blended language program.

## *Pillar 1: environments and tools for learning*

The first pillar of Blin et al. (2016) focuses on the need for creating environments and using learning tools that offer utility and flexibility. As discussed, the choice to use the LMS as the main mode of lesson instruction was motivated by a need to fulfil the National Standards (Australian Government, Federal Registration of Legislation, 2018) that require no less than 100 hours (about four days) of self-access study materials be provided to the students. As Ethan revealed, the program saw that applying a 'flipped classroom' approach could be the most effective way to meet the requirement as lesson content is designed in such a way that students learn material that they can access at any time (Rabidoux & Rottmann, 2018; Chen Hsieh, Wen-Chi Wu, & Marek, 2017). To check compliance, students could then be assessed. Teachers, however, told us that they saw limitations in such an approach.

For the teachers, the use of a flipped approach fostered a non-communicative, passive classroom. Perhaps, as was apparent in the analysis of interviews, the key issue was an over-reliance on material presentations through slides. According to Jennifer, students tended to disengage when they encountered slides; for the students, slides were seen to be 'input'. Besides slides, however, Charles suggested that other self-access materials such as videos caused students to work in isolation:

> It does feel a little bit like a buzzword in that, great, that means they can do stuff for homework but the lessons aren't necessarily being developed. For me, if it's a flipped classroom then they do, because the whole material on LMS is designed to be done individually and then there are tasks that we have developed that they're gonna come do in the classroom.
>
> (Charles, Int. 01, Lines 93–94)

> For example, in a classroom it might say watch this little clip and do this discussion then do this quiz. If you try to do that in class you've got all the students sitting there like this with different videos all going at the same time and they're plugging in this quiz then it gives them the answer and there's no real . . . it becomes a very non-communicative classroom.
>
> (Charles, Int. 01, Line 30)

Because students were able to access information from slides and videos independently, they may have felt that they did not need to pay attention to the teacher. In other words, the input may be there, but there does not seem to be an application and extension of that input during face-to-face class sessions.

Interviews with three teachers showed that each had a different interpretation of what a flipped approach entails. However, the consensus was that lesson materials are designed in such a way that students have ready access to some type of input (such as assigned readings or videos explaining a certain concept) from which they are to do independent study or preparatory revision at home. With the assumption that students have gone through the necessary input prior to class, students would be more prepared for the face-to-face class sessions where they would demonstrate their understanding of the lesson content through activities involving oral or written application tasks. In other words, there should be a logical extension from the tasks students do at home to their application in the classroom, ideally involving face-to-face components. At the time of this study, however, according to interviews with the teachers, implementing a flipped classroom approach seemed to be an avenue where unfinished tasks were then assigned as homework, which may or may not have been extended in the next face-to-face session.

Teachers also noted that the flipped approach encouraged self-access study; as a result, students focused on their own devices during face-to-face class sessions and did not like activities that did not revolve around technology. Although self-access study materials may well lead to greater student autonomy (Hinkelman, 2018), it appears that 'too much' of an emphasis on technology runs the risk of devaluing the face-to-face elements of blended designs. Excerpts from interviews with Jennifer and Sophia illustrate teacher concerns:

> I think some things have worked really well and others haven't, but I think that for me the negative mainly would be that students are focused too much on their tablet computers really . . . we've got to work out how to best vary activities so that there's some time away from the tablet computer. Sometimes there's a real communicative need . . . that I think we've really got to think about.
>
> (Jennifer, Int. 01, Lines 122 and 135)

> You then have to make a conscious effort to . . . get them up and moving and doing other things and working with paper . . . so it's not just totally attached to their tablet computers. Because I mean you know it's unhealthy and that's not sustainable . . . but I think you know it's unethical [that] . . . they have to do everything through a tablet computer.
>
> (Sophia, Int. 01, Line 113)

Although the teachers seem to be concerned solely with 'device' perspectives and not a 'system thinking' view, their thoughts highlight a general instructor resentment that places an emphasis on technology and creative lesson planning. To illustrate, Jennifer described her use of online quizzes in class as not "[knowing] what to do as a teacher, really . . . they've done the quiz, checked their answers and then we just sit there . . ." (Jennifer, Int. 01, Lines 129–130). She explained that the pedagogical value of discussing the answers together as a class was lost because students often already knew the answer in advance; further, limits of the technology made it difficult to project responses on a shared classroom screen.

Overall, the language teachers felt that blended approaches required more thoughtful lesson design and conscious decision making. Thoughtful lesson design (as opposed to mere materials development) involves, they suggested, not simply viewing the materials as stand-alone input but examining how each component connected with others that resulted in a varied set of learning outcomes. The teachers argued that face-to-face sessions should emphasise communicative activities and that active learning tasks involve only minimal, or even no, use of technology.

## *Pillar 2: pedagogical and professional development*

Under their second pillar of pedagogical and professional development, Blin et al. (2016) see a need for the capacity building of teachers to promote sustainable teaching practices. Based on our document analysis of the LMS materials, much of the materials highlighted content rather than drew attention to language development. Teachers confirmed our conclusion:

> Just the material we're trying together, often like with listening or readings, there's a bunch of quiz questions that someone's made but . . . that's just comprehension. What are the skills that we're teaching them around these kind of electronic videos and things that we've made, like it often just seems like we're throwing content at them but without really a thought of how, what exactly are we learning here, you know?
>
> (Charles, Int. 01, Lines 49–50)

> It's not very systematic, no. So, we're all feeling a bit like we're pulling . . . we're sort of feeling a bit bad about not teaching enough grammar so we're pulling it out of the air a bit and . . . that needs to be addressed somehow in the next revision of the course.
>
> (Sophia, Int. 01, Line 78)

Issues surrounding the presence of more content rather than language skills may point to a lack of professional development. The conflicts between these two pillars can be attributed to teachers not having the knowledge or skills to design lessons suitable for an online format. This is a recurring theme in blended research: teachers need to be given proper training on how to design materials and lessons based on sound pedagogy, leading to more informed decisions in lesson design (McGill, Klobas, & Renzi, 2014). Exposing teachers to the relevant theoretical underpinnings helps them to link theory with practice, enables them to justify the rationale behind each lesson they create, and helps them keep abreast of the latest changes in technology (Brečko, Kampylis, & Punie, 2014).

Our analysis revealed a need to consider aspects of time, whether length of service, release time, or the coordination of similar activities. Length of service matters; as noted by Charles, the new status of most staff had a negative effect on the program:

> Virtually the entire team was brought in new, so there was something like 17 out of 20, maybe 19, teachers and something like 15 of us had never worked at Royal College before, and the other few had come just

for August Intensive for six months and then [were] gone and I don't think there were any ongoing staff among our team.

(Charles, Int. 01, Line 10)

Learning to work with colleagues from different working backgrounds and with differing experience can complicate intense collaborative work such as materials development, particularly under deadlines (Singh & Hardaker, 2014). Not only do teachers have to adjust to varying approaches to materials development work, but they also must adjust to other teachers' various perspectives and pace when it comes to accomplishing any given task (Bennett, Lockyer, & Agostinho, 2018).

Secondly, teachers felt they were given too little time to produce materials and lessons. As the teachers noted, there was a gap of about four weeks between the completion of one Intensive to another; during this period, the teachers assumed that they would have time to refine existing course content and prepare for a new group of students. The push to make an entirely new set of materials for the Curriculum Review Project, however, meant that teachers only had ten working days to create materials for an incoming student cohort. As Sophia says, such time pressure caused lots of frustration because

> the modules [are] being written so close to time. You know we're not aware of what's coming up . . . so [materials are] not really prepared for it at all. . . . It's kind of day to day.
>
> (Sophia, Int. 01, Line 105)

In addition to a pressured development effort, teachers were also asked to participate in committee work to facilitate the coordination of materials development during this period. Teachers reacted badly to the extra workload entailed by administration and development:

> This word of 'innovation' you know gets thrown around a lot and should be, we should be really innovative but at the moment I don't always feel that it is . . . because there's just not that timeline and there's not enough time to develop resources that are really rich.
>
> (Charles, Int. 01, Lines 145–146)

> However, what I have not loved is the enormous time pressure to do it while you're teaching . . . everything else just keeps on going. And you know you've got to be prepared for class and students' work and all that sort of thing but fit in doing this materials development which if you . . . in my view if you do it well, it's very, very time consuming.
>
> (Jennifer, Int. 01, Line 14)

### Pillar 3: community and knowledge building

The third pillar rests on the need for teachers to collaborate and pool their resources. In the LMS Materials Development Project, how did the teachers build a community of practice as they worked towards a common goal? In addition, through the LMS project, knowledge can be built which includes all the lesson materials that teachers developed, as well as the lessons gained from undertaking this project. Taken together, then, maintaining the pillar of community and knowledge building can help with sustainability; that is, if teachers are given the opportunity to discuss their experiences and share their views of the project, feedback sessions can help in the refinement of materials development.

From the start, it is worth noting that the system was designed hierarchically, requiring teachers to follow the structure when they sought to add content. Such inflexibility left little room for teachers to experiment or change lessons without repeating the steps once material was hosted on the platform. The perceived lack of user-friendly features discouraged teachers from collaborative revisions of materials, as Sophia suggests:

> The thing is . . . that freedom has been taken away from us quite a lot so we haven't put any materials on as such as a group of teachers because it's now been designed in a way that you can't add anything. We had more freedom to just put our own stuff up before.
>
> (Sophia, Int. 01, Line 102)

As observed by Stern and Willits (2011), systems offer can offer a place to host large repositories of materials but nonetheless can limit instructor creativity and motivation. For his part, Charles recalled his experience teaching in two differing program intakes. In the second intake, he noted that there was less sharing of resources, but he thought it was caused by factors not directly related to the LMS alone:

> And we don't, we just don't have time to collaborate that much. There hasn't been as much sharing of resources this time as there was last time between teachers or talking about what you're doing because there's all these meetings, committee meetings. And then there's the rush to create materials.
>
> (Charles, Int. 01, Line 133)

Sophia (Int. 01, Line 102) also explains that prior to the change in the LMS being the main mode of lesson instruction, the Intensive intake teachers worked more collegially, using a shared drive to contribute materials. In the shared drive, all teachers could access any of the materials and adapt them for their own use. The lack of a single designated platform, it appears, gave the teachers greater freedom to interpret the curriculum in ways that suited their own individual teaching styles.

In contrast, Jennifer suggested that the LMS created more opportunities for teachers to discuss and refine a range of materials:

> It's just a huge variation . . . but part of a good thing is that because . . . people are forced to talk to each other quite a lot about how they use that or you know how this could be improved so I actually reckon that's quite good thing . . . that we are sort of collaborating a little bit more.
>
> (Jennifer, Int. 01, Line 155)

In our analysis, we saw that the discrepancy in perception related to the different interpretations that teachers held about collaboration. For Charles and Sophia, collaboration meant that teachers pooled their resources on a familiar shared drive; for Jennifer, the dual challenges of learning an LMS while at the same time creating new materials brought instructors more in line with one another.

These accounts of teachers' diverse experiences and expectations of technology show how it influences their work in community and knowledge-building practices. As we have seen, the interactions between the two pillars of technology and community affect the manner and frequency in which teachers collaborate with one another. On the one hand, it appears that the inherent inflexibility of the LMS hampered teachers' willingness to share resources; on the other hand, however, it was the very challenges of using the more hierarchical system of the LMS that encouraged more collaboration amongst teachers.

### *Pillar 4: organisational structures*

To reiterate, the EAP Intensive course underwent a major redevelopment as a precursor to the broader Curriculum Review Project that affected each of the cohorts, intakes, and staff of the program. At the end of the projects' pre-planning stage, a meeting was held among the EAP Intensive teachers to identify the graduate attributes and objectives of the new curriculum. Based on these graduate attributes and course objectives, a syllabus was then created that consisted of six modules. It is from these six modules that teachers had to design lesson materials and create assessment tasks. As we analysed the data that was gathered during this period, four themes emerged in relation to organisational structures.

The first theme that our analysis revealed was the importance of attending to the power relations between the program coordinator (Ethan) at the meso level, and the teachers at the micro level. Being competent both with the system and materials design, Ethan is an important actor (Selwyn, 2013) in the LMS Capacity Building Project system, particularly in his role as the technology 'champion' (Heaton-Shrestha, May, & Burke, 2009). Technology championscan lead technology adoption by example as well as provide skills training, so they are especially important in ensuring the uptake of technology within institutions. Ethan, too, held a management role that could help to foster a culture of blended learning approaches. Capacity building of teachers is crucial to sustainable practices (Kennedy & Levy, 2009).

Although Ethan's role as program coordinator was indeed crucial, it also revealed issues that often surround relationships of power. Based on interview accounts, teachers were not convinced that the hierarchical structure of the LMS offered a great deal of flexibility. In his role as program coordinator, Ethan compounded their dislike of the structure as he promoted a model lesson for teachers to follow "in the format that [he] wanted on the LMS" (Charles, Int. 01, Line 70). Because the model came from the program coordinator, teachers thought that it had to be followed. According to Charles (Int. 01, Line 151), teachers produced designs to meet Ethan's approval, not lessons that they themselves thought were truly suitable. Here, then, perceived limitations of the technology are negatively compounded by power and organisational structure.

Due to hierarchical structures within the EAP program, it is unsurprising that the teachers, being in a more subordinate position, followed the format prescribed by the program coordinator. However, this issue was also exacerbated by two contributing factors. The first factor is the fact most of the teachers were not as well versed as Ethan in materials design or operating in the Moodle environment. Therefore, they might have found it easier to follow the model, instead of spending time trying more creative ways of presenting the input or producing more varied tasks. The second issue is the time pressure of producing materials. While teachers may be able to learn the technical skills on their own, they simply do not have enough time to do so. Therefore, not having as much technical knowledge as Ethan might have affected teachers' confidence to experiment with alternative designs or content beyond the model provided.

These factors suggest that power relations affect sustainability in that following a prescribed model may mean a lack of ownership of the materials designed as they may not be based on what the teacher felt was appropriate. It may even be the case that the teachers involved are designing materials based on someone else's vision or pedagogical beliefs, which they may not share or may even disagree with. Therefore, teachers may lack a sense of ownership in the design process. They may have been given the opportunity to create and design materials as they saw fit, but due to the factors mentioned previously, they may just design based on the model. Indirectly, this issue of power relations may affect the emotional investment teachers have towards the designed materials, how vested they are in the use of the LMS, and whether they will continue to use the technology in their own teaching.

On a related issue, interview data also revealed that lesson material that some teachers developed mostly using a shared drive application had somehow undergone major revisions through the process of translating the material into an online format and subsequently uploaded to the LMS. In other words, final versions that were published on the LMS did not match the teacher's original vision or interpretation of the content. Such movement caused frustration for teachers who felt it disheartening to spend hours developing materials only to see them be changed beyond what they had originally intended. Teachers felt that it was a waste of time especially since they used personal time to prepare lesson materials to meet a given deadline. Thus, the issue of power relations is indirectly related to trust. Although teachers were given the task of developing materials, their work always required further approval and some modification. The theme of power relations illustrates how elements within the pillar of environments and tools for learning can lead to conflict within the pillar of organisational structures.

As discussed, the hierarchical structure of the LMS can affect the nature of materials development. First, having a model lesson developed by someone who is not only in a higher position but also technologically savvy can lead to a lack of ownership in the materials developed, as conflicts can arise between developing materials based on what teachers feel is appropriate and the tendency to conform to the model given. Another source of conflict in materials development is the transition of materials from the design to the development stage. Due to the nature of the LMS, which makes further modifications of lessons difficult after they are uploaded, teachers had to contend with instances where the lessons they had designed were changed beyond their original interpretation, leading to a waste of time and effort.

Our second theme surrounded 'expectations', or the assumptions and beliefs that program staff held regarding what is or how things should be. These expectations manifested from various sources in the organisational structure of the LMS project. One source of expectations, for example, came from Ethan, who had thought that teachers would be intrinsically motivated to learn the technical skills needed to design and upload materials onto the LMS. As expressed in an interview, Ethan thought that teachers would regard LMS project work as a means to align themselves with more dynamic, integrated teaching practices. While true for some, such expectations failed to account for teachers who were resistant to technology and unconvinced of its pedagogical value. Such differences in expectations illustrate the possible tensions that can occur between the pillars of pedagogical and professional development and organisational structures; that is, developing skills in LMS materials development was considered as an avenue for teachers to enhance their pedagogical and professional development. However, conflicts in perception can arise because not all teachers are convinced of the pedagogical value of the LMS.

Besides the expectations of the program coordinator, another source of expectations came from other March Intensive teachers using the developed materials and sources. According to interview data, some teachers had come from institutions where lesson materials were provided to them in the form of traditional textbooks or other pre-existing course materials. When entering Royal College, they thus brought an expectation with them that teaching materials would be ready and 'all they had to do was teach'. A quote from Jennifer illustrates this point:

> There were quite a lot of teachers who seemed to have worked at places where things were provided like learning materials and then, um, you just have to think about how to teach it. And then others who were much more used to this kind of environment, which is really that there is an expectation that you work out how to do things yourself really.
> 
> (Jennifer, Int. 01, Line 7)

Interviews with teachers also revealed that the EAP Intensive course had a reputation for instability and had undergone several iterations prior to the current situation. Such a historical view coloured the 'reassurances' that course and materials were ready. As the program commenced, the teachers found that preparations did not meet their expectations. Following some early frustration, they then decided that they had to work together to build a solid foundation on which to build curriculum even as the course was in session.

With both historical background and the Curriculum Review Project in mind, a clear picture emerges of the enormous demands on teacher time and planning. As a result, the lesson materials were hurriedly developed with minimal refinement and feedback. Conflicts emerged amongst colleagues: teachers involved in the materials development received negative feedback from classroom instructors who had little understanding of the increasing pressures and lack of resources. Significantly, most of the teachers worked part time and used their own personal time to meet development deadlines. Thus, the fact that teachers were going beyond what was expected of them, only to be met with negative feedback from their colleagues, eroded any motivation to work on the lessons. These teachers had expected that colleagues would display tolerance and accept a lower quality of materials, but this was not the case. A quote from Jennifer sums up their frustration:

> It's more an attitude of they need or want everything provided and, you know, for example I thought I had put everything there but obviously, there was something I just didn't think of . . . because we're doing it in our spare time so often, my reaction to that will be "Go and do it yourself!", you know? Have I not done enough?
> (Jennifer, Int. 01, Lines 90–91)

Under the pillar of organisational structures, our third theme is self-organisation, which can be viewed as the emergence of patterns of behaviour exhibited by an individual person or people in a group setting in response to events or circumstances that develop naturally, without prior planning. Concepts that influence self-organisation were most notable in the way that development teams came to feel. For example, when Jennifer first started, she was motivated to help transfer existing materials into the online LMS format. However, when she realised the amount of complexity and effort needed to complete the process, she devoted herself to materials development alone and left the online work to more experienced colleagues. She told us that it would take a significant effort to learn how to produce the online component, and she was unprepared to commit to that at this point in her career.

Each team was allowed to self-organise according to the strengths and capabilities of each member. Reflecting our own experiences of working with groups of teachers, the process of self-organisation occurred tacitly without direct negotiation of member roles and responsibilities. We could see that the tacit negotiation of roles happened as members saw how one another worked and from there, formed patterns of behaviour which led to various group members finally being designated as the 'materials development' person or the 'technology' person. Quotes from two interviews resonate with our own previous experiences. Charles noted it was "a very organic transition" (Int. 01, Line 72), and Jennifer said:

> So, in our little working group, there were three of us . . . we've just had to say, I do the materials, you do the technical stuff. And I really wanted to learn the technical stuff but I just had to admit early on that if I did that, then the process would be far too slow and we just wouldn't get there, so I sort of feel a bit like I've missed out on that.
> (Jennifer, Int. 01, Line 17)

A fourth theme revealed in data analysis was a lack of a clear organisational structure that shows up from the start of a macro view of the situation. At this level, two of the teachers involved in the LMS project were also involved in sub-projects at the broader Curriculum Improvement Project. As there was no systematic way of running the sub-projects, other than teachers being organised into semi-autonomous groups, this created a feeling of uncertainty as to the task distribution, the roles that each teacher took, and how they related to other members of the group. Extracts from interviews illustrate the confusion that Charles felt, which he described as a 'jungle path method of management':

> It would be nice to be able to tell you... that I have a sense of like I'm on this committee and this is how everything fits in and ... it's just kind of like slowly getting to know this wall of jungle, it feels a little bit like, rather than this clear sense of, like, these are how the committee structure works ... or oh, suddenly I'm being roped into this committee or you know ... It's a much more ... organic is the word. ... it sort of feels like the jungle path method of management sometimes.
> (Charles, Int. 01, Lines 177–179)

The meso level is the place of the LMS project itself. At this level, the lack of a designated project leader to coordinate the LMS Capacity Building Project meant that the teachers were not clear on the reporting structure and who they should turn to when faced with any issues. Although interviews with the teachers revealed that Ethan was in fact the project leader, this presented problems in terms of immediacy and access. Since Ethan was also responsible for the other intakes of the EAP, he had limited time to devote to this project and address any pressing issues. Although there was an associate program coordinator (Melissa), her role was more administrative, day-to-day running of the intake and not issues related to the LMS project. In fact, Melissa revealed that she was explicitly told not to be involved in the LMS project in any capacity, be it on the materials development or the uploading of materials, as her role was a more facilitative one. As an associate program coordinator, this led to her being 'out of the loop'.

The lack of clear organisational structures was further exacerbated by the fact that Sophia, who was heavily involved in the LMS project, gradually took on the role of the associate program coordinator. The assumption of this role may be due to her close relationship with Ethan, who spent a considerable amount of time training her on the more technical aspects of uploading materials, such as coding and HTML. It may be that through these sessions, Sophia became the go-to person for Ethan to pass on information to the other teachers. However, since her role as associate program coordinator was never formalised, she did not have the authority to make any administrative decisions or act on any issues related to the Intensive intake course.

The third category of organisational structures is at the micro level. This related to the working groups in which teachers developed materials. Because all the teachers were operating at the same level, this at times created conflict in that they did not want to appear to be stepping on one another's toes. For example, if they felt that certain materials created by another teacher were not appropriate, they were careful not to bring it up. This also created problems between those developing materials and those uploading them, as some of the materials were changed in the process. Again, the unclear delineation of roles caused difficulties, as changes were made without consultation on the part of the person doing the more technical aspects of the project.

The discussion on the fourth theme of lack of organisational structures (Pillar 4) points to interactions with the pillar of community and knowledge building (Pillar 3). Because of the tensions at various points of the organisational structure that included, for example, overlaps in curriculum development work, unclear leadership, and reporting structures, and conflicts within working groups, such tensions created dysfunction in the community and knowledge building practices amongst teachers that in turn affected the quality and implementation of the materials that were developed.

## Appraising the argument

With the completion of the first three stages of the argument-based approach, namely planning the argument, gathering the evidence, and presenting the argument, we can now move on to the final stage of the investigation. This stage entails appraising the argument based on the interrogation of sustainability as a system, outlined in the interpretive argument structure covered previously. In the initial stage of laying out the argument structure, we sought to assess the claim that technology as a system is sustainable in blended language learning programs. More specifically, the domain definition inference is founded on the warrant that the LMS provides an ideal system through which capacity building initiatives help to promote blended language learning sustainability. Four assumptions were used to establish this claim, which were that the use of the LMS (1) improves security through a centralised location of materials, (2) provides opportunities for collaboration and upskilling, (3) enables teachers to develop skills for online materials development quickly and easily, and (4) allows teachers to interpret and develop materials.

As shown from the analysis of data, the claim that technology as a system is sustainable is weak. Although the first assumption is supported by interview data that most teachers agree that the LMS provides better security, the rest of the assumptions do not support any further assumptions as complications amongst work teams, the lack of pedagogical and professional development training, and teachers' lack of expertise hampered any claims of long-term sustainability.

The second inference of evaluation is based on the warrant that the analysis identifies the institutional stance towards sustainability as a system in blended learning. In this inference, which concerns an evaluation of data collection and analysis procedures, an examination of the assumptions indicates that this inference is strong. Our study incorporates longitudinal ethnographic and participatory ethnographic research designs which increase the rigour and trustworthiness of data, through immersion in the site of study, documentation of field notes, and reflective journal insights.

The third inference requires an explanation of the findings. As discussed, data analysis provides insights which indicate that the sustainability demands of LMS have not been fully met. The explanation inference is based on the warrant that the findings are consistent with an understanding of the context of the case study. The key assumption for this inference is that sustainability, enacted through the teachers' capacity building, is a goal of the institution. Another key assumption is that the intended use of the LMS is understood by all stakeholders. As shown in the findings of this case study, the assumptions were not supported by the evidence: that is, as the technology training needs of teachers proved to be too demanding, initiatives to promote sustainability using the LMS have not reached long-term viability.

The claim that the LMS fosters capacity building and thus sustains blended language learning is weak; that is, the notion that the LMS is instrumental in fostering sustainable blended learning through capacity building initiatives has not been supported and thus could be refuted. More specifically, in line with Golonka, Bowles, Frank, Richardson, and Freynik (2014), any notion that the LMS is a key component of blended language learning sustainability would be regarded as 'moderate'. Here, while the first two inferences of domain definition and evaluation were met, there is insufficient evidence to fully support either the explanation or utilisation inferences. With regard to sustainability as a system, the explanation inference rests on the assumption that stakeholders understand the intended use of the LMS. However, interview data has shown that teachers were not fully clear on what the primary use of the LMS was. As for the utilisation inference, we cannot assess whether the findings of our study will encourage key stakeholders to improve sustainable practices.

## Summary of the chapter

Determining the sustainability of the LMS as a system is crucial if it is to be used effectively in the long term. By structuring this case study within the interpretive argument framework (Gruba et al., 2016) and analysing the data through the lens of blended learning sustainability (Blin et al., 2016), a case can be built to determine whether the claim that the LMS promotes sustainability is weak, moderate, or strong.

From the analysis of data emerging from the four pillars, we can conclude that the key issues relate to resistance, power, relationships, and timing, all of which do not relate much to technology, but more to the actors (Selwyn, 2013) using such technology. Therefore, by focusing on and identifying the issues of the LMS as a system, this investigation revealed breakdowns within the broader organisation. More specifically, adopting a view of the LMS as a technological system identified weaknesses in the socio-cultural aspects of the EAP department in the process of LMS project implementation. Similarly, by viewing technology as a system of inter-related components, once the problems are identified, certain changes need to be made to bring about the desired outcomes.

One theme that emerged in the use of the LMS was timing. For example, rather than having teachers develop teaching materials to be used as the course progressed, more time could have been allocated for the proper design and hosting of materials so that the implementation of the project could run more smoothly. Consequently, factoring in the limited time available may have meant choosing not to fully implement the LMS as the recent technology even as more students were arriving. Another aspect of timing was the involvement of teachers in the Intensive intake under the Curriculum Improvement Projects. These layers of extra duties and fragmenting of focus across different projects while also teaching appeared to exacerbate time constraints for the teachers. Another aspect of timing is giving teachers enough time to get used to using the LMS in a more nuanced way through the development of materials. As mentioned, teachers did use the LMS previously, but this was limited to the creation of folders which teachers used to organise their materials.

How might our findings contribute to the long-term sustainability of the system? In our view, a greater focus on and support for meso-level program leadership would help to foster sustainability. As we have seen, macro-level directives got the LMS underway and, conversely, we have long understood as a field that micro-level teacher professional development and classroom support is needed (Bennett et al., 2018). What is often missing, though, is support for the meso level. Accordingly, we encourage meso-level leaders to attend professional development workshops; all too often, we suggest, professional development opportunities target classroom instructors. What can we do to support program leadership? For starters, we think that leaders need assistance in developing a better understanding of educational systems; that is, they may need to gain insight that what happens to one component of the project can adversely affect the outcomes of other components and the project. Further, program leadership may need help as they set out a clear structure and plan for the role of the LMS materials within the wider blended learning system. Again, they need to be able to make informed decisions regarding lesson design and materials development. In the same vein, program leaders may require assistance in clarifying roles and responsibilities of their own staff such that teachers understand the expectations placed on them and how to relate to other members of the committee.

In summary, what is most striking from the case study findings is that issues of sustainability, as defined in our work, concern more managerial/administrative issues as opposed to technological limitations. From a systems perspective, once the problems are identified, certain changes need to be made to the system to bring about the desired outcome. For example, under the theme of timing, where teachers were developing materials as the course progressed, more time could have been allocated for the proper design and hosting of materials. Our analysis of the issues faced during the two LMS projects has led me to conclude that the system view of technology was unsustainable and thus a more viable form of technology was required. Our next chapter presents a third case study which narrows the view of technology to an application perspective.

## References

Arnold, R. D., & Wade, J. P. (2015). A definition of systems thinking: A systems approach. *Procedia Computer Science, 44*, 669–678. doi:10.1016/j.procs.2015.03.050

Australian Government, Federal Register of Legislation. (2018). *ELICOS (English Language Intensive Courses for Overseas Students) Standards 2018.* www.legislation.gov.au/Details/F2017L01349

Banathy, B. H., & Jenlink, P. M. (2004). Systems inquiry and its application in education. In D. H. Jonassen (Ed.), *Handbook of research on educational communications and technology* (2nd ed., pp. 37–57). Lawrence Erlbaum.

Bax, S. (2011). Normalisation revisited: The effective use of technology in language education. *International Journal of Computer-Assisted Language Learning and Teaching, 1*(2), 1–15.

Bennett, S., Lockyer, L., & Agostinho, S. (2018). Towards sustainable technology-enhanced innovation in higher education: Advancing learning design by understanding and supporting teacher design practice. *British Journal of Educational Technology, 49*(6), 1014–1026.

Blin, F., Jalkanen, J., & Taalas, P. (2016). Sustainable CALL development. In F. Farr, & L. Murray (Eds.), *The Routledge handbook of language learning and technology* (pp. 223–238). Routledge.

Brečko, B. N., Kampylis, P., & Punie, Y. (2014). *Mainstreaming ICT-enabled innovation in education and training in Europe: Policy actions for sustainability, scalability, and impact at system level.* Publications Office of the European Union. https://publications.jrc.ec.europa.eu/repository/handle/JRC83502

Chen Hsieh, J. S., Wen-Chi Wu, V., & Marek, M. W. (2017). Using the flipped classroom to enhance EFL learning. *Computer Assisted Language Learning, 30*(1–2), 1–21. doi:10.1080/09588221.2015.1111910

Demirkan, H. (2010). A reference model for sustainable e-learning service systems: Experiences with the Joint University/Teradata Consortium. *Decision Sciences Journal of Innovative Education, 8*(1), 151–189.

Golonka, E. M., Bowles, A. R., Frank, V. M., Richardson, D. L., & Freynik, S. (2014). Technologies for foreign language learning: A review of technology types and their effectiveness. *Computer Assisted Language Learning, 27*(1), 70–105. doi:10.1080/09588221.2012.700315

Gruba, P., Cardenas-Claros, M. S., Suvorov, R., & Rick, K. (2016). *Blended language program evaluation.* Palgrave Macmillan.

Gruba, P., & Hinkelman, D. (2012). *Blending technologies in second language classrooms.* Palgrave Macmillan.

Heaton-Shrestha, C., May, S., & Burke, L. (2009). Student retention in higher education: What role for virtual learning environments? *Journal of Further and Higher Education, 33*, 83–92. doi:10.1080/03098770802645189

Hinkelman, D. (2018). *Blending technologies in second language classrooms.* Palgrave Macmillan.

Ison, R. (2008). Systems thinking and practice for action research. In P. Reason & H. Bradbury (Eds.), *The SAGE handbook of action research: Participative inquiry and practice* (pp. 139–158). Sage.

Kennedy, C., & Levy, M. (2009). Sustainability and computer-assisted language learning: Factors for success in a context of change. *Computer Assisted Language Learning, 22*(5), 445.

Kubanyiova, M., & Crookes, G. (2016). Re-envisioning the roles, tasks, and contributions of language teachers in the multilingual era of language education research and practice. *The Modern Language Journal, 100*(S1), 117–132. doi:10.1111/modl.12304

McGill, T. J., Klobas, J. E., & Renzi, S. (2014). Critical success factors for the continuation of e-learning initiatives. *The Internet and Higher Education, 22*, 24–36.

Mele, C., Pels, J., & Polese, F. (2010). A brief review of systems theories and their managerial applications. *Service Science, 2*(1–2), 126–135. doi:10.1287/serv.2.1_2.126

Patton, M. Q. (2011). *Developmental evaluation: Applying complexity concepts to enhance innovation and use.* The Guilford Press.

Rabidoux, S., & Rottmann, A. (2018). Re-envisioning the archaic higher education learning environment: Implementation processes for flipped classrooms. *International Journal on E-Learning, 17*(1), 85–93.

Schulze, M., & Scholz, K. W. (2016). Complex adaptive systems in CALL research. In C. G. Caws & M. J. Hamel (Eds.), *Learner-computer interactions: New insights on CALL theories and applications* (pp. 65–88). John Benjamins.

Selwyn, N. (2013). *Distrusting educational technology: Critical questions for changing times*. Routledge.

Singh, G., & Hardaker, G. (2014). Barriers and enablers to adoption and diffusion of eLearning: A systematic review of the literature—A need for an integrative approach. *Education and Training, 56*(2), 105–121. doi:10.1108/ET-11-2012-0123

Stern, D. M., & Willits, M. D. D. (2011). Social media killed the LMS: Re-imagining the traditional learning management system in the age of blogs and online social networks. In *Educating educators with social media* (pp. 347–373). Emerald Insights.

Zanjani, N., Edwards, S. L., Nykvist, S., & Geva, S. (2017). The important elements of LMS design that affect user engagement with e-learning tools within LMSs in the higher education sector. *Australasian Journal of Educational Technology, 33*(1), 19–31.

# 4 The sustainability of an application in blended language programs

Following two unsuccessful attempts at technology integration, program administrators came to understand that the sustainability of their efforts would rely on syllabus integration and widespread use. They understood, too, that this third effort to blend technology must not place too much additional demands on staff. With such issues now at the forefront, program administrators turned to the integration of an application called Padlet (Jacobson, 2015) and made it clear that sustainability was now the key goal in their renewed efforts. This chapter details the efforts to integrate an application, make it sustainable, and evaluate the work of the program in achieving this goal.

## Situating the use of the application in blended language learning

Blended language learning theorists have long considered the role of applications, or software, in their discussion of open source (van Rooij, 2009), commercial suites (Levy, 2016), and web-based tools Stockwell (2016) that work through physical devices and global networks (Hinkelman, 2018). More recently, lightweight tools such as Padlet that provide both presentation and authoring capability have also been integrated in language learning.

Padlet is an online, open-source application that enables users to create, share, and collaborate in an easy and intuitive way (England, 2017). In its most basic form, Padlet can be considered as an electronic 'notice board', enabling users to compile and organise several types of online content into a sort of 'vision board' which can be made accessible for others to view, comment on, and collaborate (Fuchs, 2014). According to Padlet, the application offers ease of use, compatibility with a wide range of file types and devices, visual appeal, flexibility, and accessibility; a no-cost, limited version can be downloaded with options to upgrade to versions suited for school and business purposes.

DOI: 10.4324/b22794-4

Due to its customisability and ease of use, Padlet has been used in many pedagogical applications. In the specific context of English as a Foreign Language (EFL), England (2017) provides a brief overview of Padlet, gives instructions on how to use the application, discusses its pedagogical uses in the ESL/EFL context, and concludes with its limitations. Overall, teachers have used Padlet for sharing information, facilitating brain-storming, and as an accessible repository for supplementary resources (England, 2017). Much like Fuchs (2014), England suggests that Padlet increases student motivation and interest through interactive activities that include using online discussion boards to post book reviews to be shared, read, and commented on by teachers and other students. England (2017) notes challenges, too, that must be addressed prior to integration: time to adjust to the technology, unreliable internet connectivity, a need to monitor student discussions, and the related long-standing issues of privacy and copyright.

Directly relevant to the present study, Lahlafi and Rushton (2015) provide a study of the use of Padlet in a blended academic pathway course that was designed to enhance the academic literacy skills of international students. As detailed in their study, students used Padlet as an online "wall" to share and analyse course-related information. For example, teachers would create a Padlet wall to post questions such as the meaning of a peer-reviewed journal article as a prompt for students to discuss and respond by posting their answers. In addition to facilitating such workshop activities, Padlets were also used for post-course evaluation purposes where students share their thoughts on what they learned both during and after the course. Survey and interview results showed staunch support for the application, as 72% of students planned to continue using Padlet for future presentation tasks and 21% of the students reported that its novelty fostered their interest in mobile language learning and facilitated online interactivity (Lahlafi & Rushton, 2015).

Graham (2014) provides another example of the use of Padlet in an academic literacy context. To address students' tendency not to use social media platforms for academic purposes, the study explored the ability of Padlets to motivate student engagement outside of face-to-face sessions. Students had resisted the use of social media to date because of a lack of a clear incentive (not being a compulsory or graded task), and a need to draw clear boundaries between the personal and academic aspects of their lives. Graham (2014) concluded, however, that Padlet offered a sound alternative to other social media, in that the application (1) offers a platform for creating virtual learning communities, (2) facilitates collaborative activities, and (3) features privacy settings which allow for greater control of public access to student information.

A third example of the use of Padlet in academic literacy settings can be found in Jacobson (2015), focusing on aspects of course design. Jacobson advocates the use of a flipped approach and, like England (2017), wants students to engage with introductory activities prior to attending class to stimulate their thinking about course content. As a preparatory learning task, Jacobson (2015) proposes using a Padlet wall for instructors to post lesson questions to which students can submit their responses. The inherent benefit of creating a shared online space is that students can collaborate, interact, and reflect on their responses as well as the responses of others. Such preparatory activities generate student engagement with the lesson content, allowing them to be better prepared for the extension and reinforcement tasks in face-to-face sessions.

Designed to increase information sharing and collaboration, Padlet has potential for various classroom purposes including student engagement. Fuchs (2014) states that with proper planning and implementation, Padlet can be used to enhance student participation through its capacity for anonymous posting and formative feedback. Citing common socio-cultural barriers to active class participation which range from fear of making mistakes, being misunderstood, or misjudged, feelings of powerlessness or embarrassment, to tensions in teacher-student hierarchy, Fuchs (2014) argues that conducting "graffiti wall" activities through the Padlet can be an effective way for teachers to address such challenges in that students can respond to the comments and posts of others in ways that foster greater interaction (Mallon & Bernsten, 2015; Duță & Martínez-Rivera, 2015).

Unfortunately, the integration of applications may face difficulties when they are hosted online (slow internet connectivity, website glitches, etc.) and exacerbate the uncertainties (Fuchs, 2014). In fact, Fuchs stresses that total dependency on a stable internet connection can put class activities at risk of coming to a complete standstill should the internet connection suddenly drop. Modifications to online content are updated and saved in real time in Padlets that Fuchs (2014) thought was initially an 'advantage, but later saw how it prompted a sense of immediacy that encouraged students to post irrelevant comments to gain attention. Fuchs questioned too if Padlet may be perceived as a flashy gimmick that emphasised visual appeal (colourful background, use of images as a preview of content, arrangement of content, etc.) with a focus on style over substance. Such questions, Fuchs (2014) thought, may undermine the use of Padlet for long-time pedagogical activities.

In brief, the potential affordances of Padlet include a promised ease of use, aesthetic appeal, customisability, and compatibility with a host of other applications and mobile devices, making it an attractive option that instructors can use in the classroom. Another aspect is that because Padlet is user-friendly and does not require technical expertise beyond basic computing skills, anyone, including students, can create Padlets. Thus, the locus of content creation no longer rests solely with the instructor, enabling student engagement through the process of active learning discussed previously. The online application, of course, requires a stable internet connection to be effectively used. Padlet has also been applied to a variety of contexts, including language learning and academic literacy programs.

## Planning the argument

After a review of the literature, we once again put our thoughts into an argument structure to identify warrant, assumptions, and claims regarding the sustainability of technology as an application, as shown in Table 4.1.

Briefly, Table 4.1 seeks to interrogate the central claim that the use of Padlet, as a case study application, will address sustainability issues. As shown in the earlier chapter, the use of the LMS was not sustainable in the program. Here, then, the assumptions underlying the claim was that the Padlet could be more sustainable in that it would be readily adopted by instructors, enhance collegial interactions, and fit into the EAP as a tool that could help structure lesson plans. Moving up from the domain inference, the remainder of the argument relies on sound data gathering and analysis until the eventual ramification that outcomes of the current study could be used, or potentially transferred, to similar contexts.

*Table 4.1* Inferences, warrants, and assumptions in the argument

| Inferences | Warrants and assumptions (numbered after each warrant) |
| --- | --- |
| **E. Ramification** ↑ | An interrogation of sustainability as an application advances theory development and improves approaches to the development of blended language learning. |
| | 1. The findings are transferable to similar programs. |
| | 2. The findings are disseminated in an appropriate forum. |
| | 3. Work on sustainability of applications interests the broader community. |
| **D. Utilisation** ↑ | An understanding of sustainability as an application encourages stakeholders to make use of the findings to improve the program. |
| | 1. The findings resonate and are powerful enough to stimulate action. |
| | 2. The stakeholders take ownership of the findings. |
| | 3. The stakeholders can understand the findings. |
| | 4. The findings can be used to improve issues of sustainability in the integration of technology in language learning programs. |

(*Continued*)

*Table 4.1* (Continued)

| Inferences | Warrants and assumptions (numbered after each warrant) |
| --- | --- |
| **C. Explanation** ↑ | The findings are consistent with an understanding of the context of the case study.<br>1. The intended use of the application is understood by key stakeholders.<br>2. Sustainability, enacted through the scaling of resources, is a prime goal.<br>3. Educational technology research is based on project criteria for course, professional, or theoretical development and not overall program improvement. |
| **B. Evaluation** ↑ | The analysis identifies the institutional stance towards sustainability as an application in blended learning.<br>1. The analysis is accurate, robust, and trustworthy.<br>2. The analytical processes are conducted in ways that are appropriate and ethical to the field.<br>3. Discourse analysis can identify themes regarding sustainability as a system.<br>4. The use of Padlet in the EAP program represents the area to be evaluated. |
| **A. Domain definition** ↑ | The use of Padlet as a case study application will address sustainability issues.<br>1. Padlet will be a "fit-for-purpose" pedagogical application for the EAP.<br>2. Teachers will be able to use it with minimal training.<br>3. Integration of the application will enhance collegiality.<br>4. Lesson planning will be structured through the application. |

Source: Adapted from Gruba, Cardenas-Claros, Suvorov, & Rick (2016)

## Gathering the evidence

Underpinned by an ethnographic orientation, our action research was conducted in three cycles of research as shown in Table 4.2.

As shown in Table 4.2, the first cycle involved the planning stage which included the training of teachers to use Padlet, the use of Padlet to partially develop Module 6 of the March Intensive materials which were then hosted on the LMS, and finally the full use of the Padlet by transferring the developed LMS materials into the Padlet application. The second cycle involved the continuous and concurrent work of transferring existing LMS materials (Modules 2–6) into the Padlet and further developing them, while at the

*Table 4.2* Cycles of data collection

| Cycles | Stages | Interventions |
|---|---|---|
| 1 | Planning | • Ethan trained March Intensive teachers on Padlet.<br>• Ethan asked Charles to do Module 6 materials development on Padlet and then embed the Padlet materials to LMS.<br>• After the end of March Intensive, Jennifer was asked to transfer Module 1 materials from LMS to the Padlet application.<br>• Padlet workshop was conducted during orientation session for new Intensive teachers. Four new teachers were assigned to help Jennifer in Module 1 materials.<br>• Grouping of ongoing and new teachers to work on materials for Modules 2–6.<br>• Transfer of developed materials from LMS to Padlet.<br>• Development of new Padlet materials to supplement LMS materials |
| 2 | Concurrent Materials trial/ development | • Transfer and development work of Modules 2–6 on Padlet<br>• Ongoing trialling of materials by all Intensive teachers<br>• Feedback given periodically in meetings/Padlet sessions |
| 3 | Evaluation | • Teacher feedback on materials developed<br>• Proposed changes/refinement of materials |

same teaching and trialling the materials. The trialling and feedback stage involved all August Intensive teachers. The third cycle involved the evaluation of the materials, including an informal evaluation of the Padlet as it was the main technological platform used in this phase.

As a malleable concept, the level of an evaluation can be adjusted to its context (Gruba et al., 2016) that may result in further divisions amongst the initial macro-meso-micro classification. To clarify, we see interviews conducted with EAP program administrators best placed at meso-macro level. Our purpose here, at this intermediate level, was to gain an administrative view of the decision to adopt the Padlet and how its adoption came to affect curriculum change. Next, we turned our attention to those who transit between meso and micro level and conducted interviews with three EAP teachers who act as materials developer for Padlet resources while simultaneously teaching in the EAP program.

Cynthia, as an action research ethnographer, also gathered classroom insights and experiences shared by other teachers at the meso-micro level. The first set of analysed documents is the agenda and minutes for the August Intensive meetings, which were held fortnightly. In addition to this documentation, Cynthia had access to shared folders that contained Padlet-related documents, such as teacher wikis for collating feedback and suggestions to improve Padlet materials. Additionally, she examined the Padlets themselves that were designed for either administrative or classroom purposes. Administrative Padlets were used to disseminate information about the program such as information about enrolment, class syllabus, professional development, and meetings. Classroom Padlets were designed as the main resource material for teaching and were further divided into the Main program and the Intensive program Padlets. These classroom Padlets contained the lesson modules, syllabus, course timeline, and assessment details for each program.

Finally, with a specific focus on the micro level, Cynthia made extensive field notes and reflective journal entries to understand how the Padlet was used in the classroom by herself and other teachers. Taken together, a more comprehensive picture of how Padlet has worked in the real-world context can be established by comparing the similarities and differences in our collective views and experiences. In terms of field notes (again, in an ethnographic lens), we documented insights and personal observations regarding the adoption of Padlet gathered from the meetings that Cynthia attended that included reflective journal entries that set out experiences of teaching the course. Because Cynthia occupied dual roles as teacher and researcher, her field notes and reflective journal entries are particularly valuable sources of information.

Once program leadership made a commitment to use the application, the Padlet was formally presented to teachers, who were asked to raise any concerns. Cynthia summarised their concerns for classroom (Table 4.3) and administrative (Table 4.4) Padlets.

In terms of lesson materials, Table 4.3 shows that teachers' main concerns related to issues of appropriateness, accuracy, alignment, and consistency. For appropriateness, they expected the Padlet tasks to fit with the intended learning objectives; for example, teachers saw a proposed vocabulary quiz to be unsuitable in terms of format and content. Frequent errors in module labelling and task descriptors, a second concern, confused teachers who saw failing as part of the 'technology' of the Padlet. Alignment, or the extent that lesson components worked in tandem with one another, was a concern too. Suggestions were made, for example, to break down video clips into manageable chunks so that teachers would not have to stop and pause the video during playback. Finally, teachers were concerned that classroom Padlets lacked a common template or standard.

Besides feedback on Padlet lesson materials, administrative Padlets raised teacher concerns, as shown in Table 4.4.

As shown in Table 4.4, the first area of concern for the administrative Padlets was the lack of a top-down structure to coordinate materials development work. In this context, the lack of an overall coordinator to

*Table 4.3* Summary of concerns about classroom Padlets

| Issues | Characteristics of issues | Description/example |
|---|---|---|
| Appropriateness | Extent of tasks fitting with the intended learning objective | • Vocabulary quiz format more of a 'testing' than 'learning' task<br>• Explanations used to define target vocabulary are difficult to understand |
| Terms of reference | Clarity of task descriptors/labelling under each unit | • Correct labelling needed.<br>• Task description of 'note-taking skills' assumes that this is the first time students are encountering this topic. However, it had already been introduced in Module 1. |
| Alignment | Extent to which lesson components cohere with each other | • Length of video is longer than its corresponding note-taking task.<br>• Video is too long and should be broken down into more manageable chunks. |

*Table 4.4* Summary of administrative issues

| Issues | Characteristics of issues | Description/example |
|---|---|---|
| Lack of top-down structure | Lack of overall coordinator to administer materials development work | • Lack of clear lesson flow from one section to another<br>• Replication of materials/tasks |
| Roles and responsibilities | Lack of clarity on the roles and responsibilities of working groups | • Unclear on the nature of materials development work in working groups |
| Centralised repository of resources | Lack of a common repository for teachers | • Unclear on where to go for sources |
| Teaching approach | Lack of clarity on the degree of freedom to modify the materials | • Unclear on the parameters for modifying materials |

oversee such work meant that the lesson materials lacked coherence and organisation. More specifically, the absence of a clear top-down structure led to issues in lesson flow and replication of materials/tasks, as teachers were unaware of the nature of tasks coming before or after the lessons they designed. A second related issue is the roles and responsibilities of teachers involved in various working groups. More specifically, teachers were

70  *The sustainability of an application*

unsure whether their role was to merely transfer existing materials from the LMS to Padlet or whether they were to develop new materials. Making such a distinction is justified as both have implications on the nature and degree of work involved. For example, transferring materials from one platform to another would require far less work than developing new materials. Besides sourcing for suitable input, developing new materials would also require far more time to plan, design, source, and upload to the Padlet application. A third issue, on a centralised repository for resources, related to teachers being unclear on where to go for supplementary materials. Besides management and coordination issues, the last point of discussion related to the teaching of classes and how prescriptive such teaching would be. In this context, teachers sought clear guidelines on the degree of freedom and flexibility they had when using or modifying such materials.

After a series of informal discussions about the application, Cynthia found that teachers had legitimate concerns about Padlet lesson materials, the administration of materials development work, and the degree of flexibility. Of note, many teachers were new to the EAP program, and they were positive about technology integration. Significantly, they expected glitches at the start but felt that materials could easily be further refined in the coming semester. One extract from her field notes illustrates Cynthia's impressions at that time:

> Overall, the new teachers seem to be enthusiastic about the use of Padlet but raised many concerns as well. They also made many helpful suggestions on areas of improvement which Sophia welcomed and promised to pass along to Ethan.
> Field notes (impromptu Padlet briefing session, 23 August 2017)

Such notes were then coded and placed into themes to present the argument.

## Presenting the argument

Having gathered the evidence, we now turn to presenting the argument. Framed by the four pillars of sustainable blended learning (Blin, Jalkanen, & Taalas, 2016), evidence to support or refute claims regarding the sustainability of Padlet is presented with reference to our analysis of semi-structured interviews, document analysis, field notes, and reflective journal entries.

### *Pillar 1: environments and tools for learning*

How do environments and tools for learning relate to a program's technology integration practices, and how do such practices affect sustainability? Analysis of the data revealed that the aesthetic appeal of Padlet negatively affects its pedagogical worth; in other words, the use of the colourful application devalues its potential in teaching and learning. As argued by Fuchs (2014), a focus on visual aesthetics may lead critics to dismiss an application that favours style over substance. On the surface, new lesson materials initially gave the impression that the program was offering a dynamic, exciting curriculum but it readily became apparent that the Padlet was not sophisticated enough to meet the pedagogical demands of a tertiary language program.

Building on earlier concepts, an analysis in Table 4.5 of reflective journal entries shows how issues recurred throughout the introduction and use of the application.

*Table 4.5* Comparison of feedback on Padlet materials

| Issues | Definition | Evidence from reflective journal entries ||
| --- | --- | --- | --- |
| | | Teacher concerns | Ethnographic observations |
| Appropriateness | Extent to which tasks fit with the intended learning objective | • Issues with vocabulary quiz in terms of format and definitions of target vocabulary | • Too many activities, too little time/benefit<br>• Overlap in tasks/objectives |
| Terms of reference | Accuracy of task descriptors/labelling under each unit | • Labelling of items<br>• Task descriptions are unsuitable | • Terms of reference—labelling of lesson components not streamlined—use of related image/visual to refer to task/input |
| Alignment | Extent to which lesson components cohere | • Length of video is unsuitable | • No alignment of student proficiency and Padlet tasks<br>• No logical sequencing of Padlet tasks |
| Consistency | Lack of standardised lesson content | • Inconsistent lesson content and guidelines on "remaking" Padlets | • Inconsistencies in Padlet content/contribute/revisions<br>• Inconsistencies in the placement of Padlets |

As shown in Table 4.5, issues that first appeared in the earlier Padlet briefings recurred as the program progressed. In terms of appropriateness, additional insights from reflective journal entries showed the lack of strong lesson designs. Alongside too many activities and tasks that produced little benefit, an overlap in objectives disrupted smooth class implementation. Unfortunately, the poor labelling of lesson components into modules, units, and tasks also caused problems. As a "work around" tactic, teachers used related visual imagery to refer to the targeted input/task. A third issue on alignment revealed a mismatch between student proficiency and Padlet tasks, where tasks were either too difficult for lower-level students or too easy for higher-level students. Additionally, issues of alignment were also evident in the lack of logical sequencing among tasks. Cynthia soon discovered that different teachers did different things within the same program, and such differences caused interpersonal conflicts amongst the staff. To compound issues, the Padlets were not logically filed in named folders of the shared drive.

Adding to concerns of alignment and proficiency level, for example, the actual use of the application in blended language classrooms was beset with issues, as shown in Table 4.6.

As summarised in Table 4.6, four themes were identified in our analysis of the blended classroom implementation of the application. Although these were expected, teachers nonetheless highlighted their frustrations with the technology. Difficulties in using the application that took away from actual teaching time included issues in the application design, the use of Padlet on tablet computers, and faulty internet/Wi-Fi. The inferior quality of the application design meant that teachers had to know the correct configuration of settings and frequently refresh pages. Such disruptions hurt a smooth class implementation. A limited functionality of the Padlet application on the tablet computer, when compared to the web version, in terms of both content arrangements and tablet hardware limitations, also affected classroom implementation of activities. Though not strictly an application issue, unreliable internet connection resulted in activities coming to a complete standstill when the Padlet was used to host all lesson materials. Such interruptions then required teachers to produce a back-up plans or activities, diminishing their trust in the technology.

Similarly, teachers were forced to improvise during class when the application or its associated technology did not function well. Such impromptu class adjustments resulted in a need for teachers to constantly think on their feet to adapt; fatigue, however, led many teachers to avoid glitches as they resorted to providing paper handouts or conducting group discussions orally, instead of through a Padlet wall. Glitches compounded already existing issues of time management. In the overall curriculum, planned

*Table 4.6* Summary of issues with classroom implementation

| Theme | Characteristics of theme | Description/examples |
| --- | --- | --- |
| Technology issues | Effort needed for technology issues takes away from actual teaching time | • Technical issues with Padlet<br>• Configuration of settings<br>• Issues with content display, need to constantly refresh the page<br>• Issues with Padlet on tablet computers<br>• Tablet application of Padlet has limited functionality compared to web version<br>• Location of icons/arrangement of Padlet is different on tablet computer and laptop<br>• Tablet has oversensitive screen, limited screen space makes mind-mapping activities difficult<br>• Issues with Wi-Fi/internet connection<br>• Drops in internet connection mean class comes to a standstill<br>• Requires teachers' quick thinking to produce a back-up plan/activity |
| Need for lesson improvisations | Impromptu class adjustments that teachers make in response to issues that come up during class | • Many examples showing that teachers need to constantly think on their feet to adapt to any circumstance<br>• Technology glitches<br>• Padlet application glitches<br>• Information/task overload<br>• Tasks that don't work during class implementation |
| Need for teacher control | The need for teachers to regain a sense of control of lesson content/ student access | • Teachers don't feel 'on top' of things because the amount of Padlet content can be overwhelming<br>• Some teachers want more control so they remake the lesson Padlet every week |
| Lack of student engagement | Active student participation in their learning | • Student experiences with technology relate more to frustration than engagement<br>• The mismatch between teacher and student perception of what makes an 'engaging' task |

activities looked feasible on paper, but in actual usage teachers often needed to skip activities so that neither they nor the students became overwhelmed. Attempts to repair glitches "on the fly" often revealed that materials had been improperly stored on shared drives.

Issues also arose concerning the teacher control of lesson materials. Because the application does not restrict ways to configure text and media files, the display of Padlet content can be overwhelming. As noted in teacher interviews and personal experience, there was a sense of not being "on top of things" in terms of having a firm grasp of lesson materials. Unlike working with the LMS, where access to lesson materials was systematic, the Padlet application does not have an inherent hierarchical system of organising content. To regain a sense of control, teachers took it upon themselves to create weekly Padlets for their own classes. Significantly, the teachers did not share their own materials with others.

Perhaps because of its dynamic visual appeal, the Padlet often gave an initial impression that its use alone could motivate student learning; that is, the application was new, exciting, and full of potential. However, within a few weeks of its use, teachers began to question the pedagogical value of material designed to be 'fun' that did not seem to contribute significantly to student learning. In interviews during this time, teachers suggested that the application had more style than substance; comparably, discussions with students revealed that they too were more frustrated than engaged with the technology.

## *Pillar 2: pedagogical and professional development*

As we discussed earlier, the main reason that program leaders adopted the Padlet was that they assumed it would place far less demand on teachers. Such perception of the ease of use was based on features that included built-in Padlet templates that could be modified with simple input (such as descriptive/instructional text) and a corresponding file (such as images, videos, or documents), and a 'remake function' that allowed duplicates of existing Padlets to be modified easily if necessary. Such features gave the impression to program leadership that no professional development was required:

> In terms of scalability, this is something you can add or augment really, really quickly. To actually add a new lesson or module, we don't have to look for specialised images because it's all linked off publicly accessible materials. If teachers can figure out how to write a text and add a hyperlink that's all they need to learn. So, in terms of skills development or training, almost none.
>
> (Ethan, Int. 02, Lines 15.30–16.32)

It can be duplicated, changed and added to so easily so it's not a static platform. So, what we have there today, in two years our curriculum may look quite different, but we'll still be using the same platform and the same tools to deliver the content. With other things it's much harder to add or to share or to delete things so that's one thing about Padlet which I think makes it sustainable.
(Kelly, Int. 01, Lines 18.28–19.03)

With the false assumption that teacher professional development needs would be minimal, conflicts arose between program leadership and instructors. Our analysis showed that teachers readily found training insufficient but perceived that it was needed to use the application effectively in the classroom. According to one teacher, Jennifer, only one Padlet workshop of an hour and 30 minutes was conducted ahead of implementation. She suggested that the workshop "needed to be slower and have a follow-up session" (Jennifer, Int. 02, Line 17.02) as she witnesses a long continuum of staff competency with technology:

To me it was that sense of, right, I've showed you, therefore you can do it. There was a lot crammed in that session which was quite well-organised and prepared, but to me it was an awful lot to take in at one time. I think it was too much in that we were just introducing this whole new thing that our whole course is based on, so to me one and a half hours wasn't quite enough.
(Jennifer, Int. 02, Lines 17.57–18.58)

Jennifer's account resonated with Cynthia, who also saw a need for continuous professional development; ideally, Cynthia wrote in her journal, workshops dedicated to the fundamentals of Padlet would be provided alongside a continuing series of training sessions that help teachers cope with ongoing glitches in the classroom. An extract from her field notes summarises the key issues that arose:

Many of the questions and concerns about the technology use echo my thoughts, especially the time wasted troubleshooting problems with Padlet as well as the other platforms embedded in the application (Google Docs, LMS).
(Field notes of Intensive program meeting, August 2017)

Despite being assured that the application was easy to use and that initial issues of adjustment would diminish, a range of negative emotions began to surface as the integration continued. Teachers began to express that they had a sense of insecurity as they did not have a full understanding of Padlet, and that their own poor use of it negatively affected the students' impressions of teachers in the classroom. As noted, teachers did in fact receive some training for the application, but its limited scope and frequency meant that they had not yet mastered its effective use in the classroom. In a frank self-assessment, Jennifer revealed her embarrassment when she was unable to resolve technical issues that students encountered in class. Sophia told us that teachers said that they often felt "kind of stupid with technology" (Sophia, Int. 02); other teachers suggested that those students would become quite critical of their teachers who did not use the technology well in the classroom:

> Of course, they [students] wouldn't know what we had all gone through, but thinking, well, if they're using the technology, they should be able to use it, so why can't they?
>
> (Jennifer Int. 02, Line 43.22)

> Sometimes as a teacher it feels like as a collective of teachers, we're just trying to get enough stuff together so that we can walk into a classroom and pretend we know what's going on.
>
> (Charles, Int. 02, Line 39.50)

Unsurprisingly, Cynthia felt the same way. Like many other teachers, she felt bad at not being able to use Padlet competently and entered class with feelings of unpreparedness and apprehension as she wondered whether students would detect her lack of confidence. As researcher, Cynthia had a growing awareness that such negative experiences would eventually lead to a resistance to the integration of technology.

Alongside a growing sense of professional incompetence, the teachers we interviewed began to report an increasing sense of inferiority in relation to other teachers, particularly the newly hired part-timers. Earlier, long-term teachers noted how new instructors had mastered the Padlet quite quickly, developed their own materials, and integrated in ways that were beyond expectations. In their minds, the long-term teachers thought that they should be able to demonstrate equal, if not better, skilled technology use. The following interview extract illustrates this sentiment.

> I still think there's a bit of, sometimes you don't want to ask because you think everyone can do that and I'll just show myself, to the one that doesn't know. And a little bit of very unofficial comparing of ourselves to each other, like they're great at Padlet and I'm not.
>
> (Jennifer, Int. 02, Line 20.36)

In her field notes, Cynthia noted a growing disparity between new teachers who produced far more sophisticated Padlets than did the ongoing teachers. To illustrate, Charles expressed his reluctance at using the Padlet and maintained his usual teaching methods in the initial weeks of teaching. Instead of the Padlet, for example, he used applications that were familiar to him, such as Google Docs, and expressed reservations about the pedagogical value of Padlet. He did concede that Padlets may foster greater social interactions but did not see how conducting such activities using that application was any different than using cloud computing applications. We can conclude that teacher scepticism may hinder the sustainability of technology use, particularly when it comes to applications such as Padlet.

*Pillar 3: community and knowledge building*

In the third pillar of community and knowledge building for Blin et al. (2016), there is a focus on the importance of developing a shared culture of practice and promoting a unified community of knowledge builders and knowledge sharers. We identified three themes that relate how the adoption of Padlet affected the development of a knowledge community.

Disparities in the perception of ease of use amongst instructors affected the culture of the EAP teaching community. With the hire of 20 new part-time teachers to accommodate a dramatic increase in student enrolments in just five months, long-time teachers felt a shift in the uptake of technology from resistance and frustration to enthusiasm. Unlike permanent staff, new teachers saw little need for technical training and felt empowered as they explored Padlet resources, and this fuelled a renewed enthusiasm for technology integration. Jennifer notes the new teachers' positive impact on the EAP:

> When you've got a lot of positive people to collaborate, you learn huge amounts from each other. And I don't think [if] we just had our small ongoing teachers group it would have been as good.
> (Jennifer, Int. 02, Lines 21.30–21.41)

Inspired by the work of new instructors, ongoing staff began to see that the Padlet could offer more to the classroom teacher. The phenomenon of new teachers coming in and instigating a positive change in the attitude of other teachers demonstrates the powerful impact that teachers can have on one another through continuous sharing and collaborative opportunities. Furthermore, cultivating such opportunities is crucial, as teachers need to operate within a community of knowledge builders and knowledge sharers. In an interview, Sophia recommended that Padlet training be conducted with smaller groups of teachers in the form of a buddy/mentoring system and pointed to the power of informal chats to encourage one another. Slowly, the community began to demonstrate more creative and diversified Padlets that seemed to respect each teacher's thought processes and unique approaches.

Despite the positive impact of the fresh staff in the EAP teaching community, ongoing teachers noted a diminished sense of collegiality. As teachers told us in interviews, the rapid growth of the EAP program had caused staff to disperse across three buildings of classes and workspaces. Charles shared with us that he went days without seeing colleagues as there was now far less interaction. The segregation of the ongoing and new teachers created a range of issues for both groups of teachers that affected technology integration and application uptake.

As Charles noted, placing the new teachers in a room by themselves was a "big mistake from a cultural point of view because they're developing their own culture" (Charles, Int. 02, Line 39.50). Cynthia, too, felt newcomers were developing their own culture that was distinct from that of long-term staff, and she saw a widening disparity in Padlet use. Two quotes from Charles illustrate this point:

> The more we go our own way of this is how I use Padlet . . . and it's a process of exploration because we're all new to the platform, but because everything is happening all at once there's not that chance to collaborate and communicate and discuss.
> (Charles, Int. 02, Line 43.37)

> We've got all these different platforms and expectations, different understandings of what it is we are doing. We don't actually have a shared culture of learning really.
> (Charles, Int. 02, Line 28.13)

In further observations, Charles revealed that he knew that fresh staff seemed to be making their own way "partly because of survival and partly because there were no guidelines" (Charles, Int. 02, Line 40.31). As an example, he recounts inconsistencies where both groups of teachers could not have conversations about marking and leniency because of separate workspace locations. In her own field notes, Cynthia expressed concerns about how the segregation of staff was a disservice to both groups of teachers and its role in widening the gap between them. One recurring issue faced by new teachers was the need for time-sensitive information. Not present in a shared workspace, new teachers did not always have a sense of immediacy in terms of how to respond to arising issues. Cynthia, like others, realised that she needed to work things out for herself and respond to issues in ways she thought were best. Informal chats with teachers also confirmed to Cynthia that they applied a similar approach.

For their part, separated ongoing teachers lost opportunities for building their knowledge of the application. Increasingly, informal 'professional development' Padlet sharing sessions were initiated by groups of new teachers. Notably, even though they were organised ad hoc, session feedback was positive. Cynthia reports the sessions to be invaluable as she could see, and by inspired by, what other teachers were doing. She was encouraged to know that most of the issues, concerns, and questions raised mattered to all teachers. As a researcher, Cynthia saw the power of bottom-up initiatives as a factor in driving the sustainability of technology integration.

To compound a growing sense of disparity between the cultures of new and ongoing staff, long gaps in the timetables of instructors made it difficult for them to meet each other; that is, with more than four hours between classes, few teachers made use of collective workspace and offices. It was common, too, to have a 10–30-minute walk from an office to a classroom. As Cynthia recorded in her field notes, the combination of teachers' timetables and the less-than-ideal location of the workspace led to a lack of opportunities for teachers to meet, chat, and discuss their teaching experiences.

Ironically, although functions of the application make it easy to adapt lesson materials to suit diverse proficiency levels, promote teacher creativity and democratise materials development, an ability to create Padlets led to an uncontrolled proliferation of classroom materials that profoundly affected knowledge and community-building practices. Potentially, the use of Padlet may help to foster the sustainability of technology integration as it scales and is within the capacity building of teachers, yet the lack of a structured repository of resources led to a sense that the technology alone was "going to change what we do" in negative ways (Charles, Int. 04, Line 17.20) that hurt a sense of working on a single, coherent curriculum within a defined EAP program.

Due to its ease of use, teachers created their own Padlets in isolation instead of working on the core materials as a collective. As a result, the community aspect of knowledge building became fractured through the creation of individual Padlets. This undermined efforts to improve Padlet and the curriculum. Developing individual Padlets takes time and energy away from working on existing lesson materials. According to Jennifer, it is a time-consuming process to take materials from the core Padlet, develop a weekly lesson plan, and then file these lessons for the next cycle of materials development.

Besides the issue of time, Jennifer also highlighted that working on individual Padlets meant that changes were not shared with the wider community. In other words, the necessary feedback loop to improve existing materials was not generated. According to Jennifer, examples of such valuable teacher feedback include technology and curriculum/syllabus issues. Feedback should ideally be provided immediately and progressively, Cynthia wrote in her field notes, instead of waiting for the end of the course as teachers may forget. Due to a lack of clear structures for reporting such feedback, teachers who worked on their own Padlets most often did not document the Padlet's strengths, weaknesses, and suggestions for improvement. In terms of sustainability, creating a feedback loop could have been used to refine the technology and curriculum for future iterations of the Intensive program.

Another issue highlighted by teachers concerning the proliferation of Padlets is the risk of splintering the curriculum. Although Jennifer felt it was good that teachers were being creative through their Padlets, she worried that such a diverse set of materials would not equally prepare the students to succeed at the same assessment task across a range of differing learning experiences. Without the proper parameters in place for lesson modifications, teachers ran the risk of deviating too much from the original lesson materials, leading to inconsistencies with other classes. To illustrate, Charles relates how his students commented that other classes were doing different things than they were, as can be seen from the following extract:

> It's kind of a balance between LMS and Google Drive in that it has a basic plan there but because of the remaking, people are going off and doing their own thing with it . . . which is good in a sense that it needs work but students have commented that other classes are doing quite different things from them.
> (Charles, Int. 02, Lines 18.15–18.54)

Cynthia reflects on how teachers seemed to be doing their own thing, and she began to question the extent to which their Padlets were achieving the shared goals and objectives of the program. Interview data from Charles revealed similar concerns, where he argues that it is not so much an issue of diverse student experiences as it is of having the objectives, skills, and assessments clearly built into the course structure. However, according to teacher interviews, the assessments were being done as the course progressed. Therefore, such practices made it difficult to establish a macro view of the entire course, ensure that Padlet materials were aligned across classes, and prepare students for the same learning outcomes. As community and knowledge-building practices became diffuse, such accounts reflect a breakdown in this pillar. In other words, the sheer number of Padlets led to fractured understanding the EAP program. A quote from Charles summarises this point:

> As a group of teachers, we no longer have the same understanding of what it is we're doing and that makes change very hard because we're all trying to do different things within the organization.
> (Charles, Int. 02, Line 41.57)

From these accounts, interactions with the pillar of environments and tools for learning led to conflicts within the pillar of community and knowledge building. The main reason for the tensions between the two pillars is the Padlet's perceived ease of use which affected the EAP teaching community, created division between ongoing and part-time staff, and resulted in weakening the curriculum due to isolated working practices and diversity in individual Padlets. Taken together, these outcomes led to diminished community and knowledge-building. Although the application's perceived ease of use should have facilitated collaborative work, it had the opposite effect in that teachers turned to work alone on their own Padlets in ways that did not foster community or knowledge sharing.

### *Pillar 4: organisational structures*

The fourth pillar of Blin and colleagues (2016) emphasises the need for alignment and order within institutional organisational structures. Through a sense of common purpose, stakeholders can work to integrate technology in line with the broader goals of the institution in an order that is made possible by clear structures and procedures for implementation. Our analysis, however, revealed how such alignment and order can become distorted.

One theme to emerge in our analysis relates to a sense of disconnect amongst multi-level stakeholders in achieving the technology integration goals of the institution. The issues under this theme can be seen from several aspects. The first aspect involves meso-level stakeholders and the lack of a shared vision with regard to the place and role of technology in the EAP program. Analysis of interview data with program administrators and teachers revealed an apparent lack of clarity regarding the rationale of using applications such as Padlet in the EAP program. To illustrate, although Padlet is an effective tool for collaborative activities such as posting comments on a shared wall, teachers did not know how to extend the pedagogical application of such activities beyond encouraging student interaction. The following extracts illustrate this issue:

> I'd rather actually they have a discussion and report back on the discussion so that it can virtually keep going. I actually often don't know what

to do with that [Padlet wall discussions] because you don't want to go through every one, it would take too long and they'd get a bit bored.

(Jennifer, Int. 02, Lines 1.08.03–1.08.18)

... or [I] just have to see it as a fluency activity and nothing about grammar or language or to pick up some common mistakes. Perhaps that's why I've avoided it as well because I don't quite know what to do with those discussions yet.

(Sophia, Int. 02, Lines 16.54–17.20)

While teachers were unclear about the role of the application from a pedagogical standpoint, program administrators stressed that the Padlet was an effective platform for hosting program materials and fostered program coherence. The program administrators held a macro view of Padlet, with a focus on its administrative capabilities, whereas teachers held a micro-level view of how Padlet is situated in terms of classroom applications. In other words, teachers' concerns relate to the potential pedagogical extension of Padlet, instead of its capacity to manage the various aspects of the EAP Intensive course. This sense of disconnect may explain why teachers and program administrators may be at odds regarding the adoption of the Padlet and its capacity to add value to teaching and learning. In turn, such a disconnect at the departmental level affects sustainability in that teachers and administrators do not have a shared understanding of the manner and extent of Padlet integration in the EAP program.

The sense of disconnect amongst meso-level stakeholders was also apparent as teachers felt a lack of institutional support. Although Royal College encouraged the use of technology at the macro level and had IT units with support staff, such encouragement was not translated into teacher support for materials development work. Sophia and Charles, for example, found that teachers were working in increased isolation without the support of technological expertise or qualified curriculum/assessment writers to produce a quality program. Sophia told us in interviews that she did seek the help of IT staff beyond simple technical assistance but had found assistance to be of little use. The perceived lack of technical support can be attributed to conflicting views in organisational roles, where the technology support units may not view materials development work as part of their job specifications.

The disparity of perspectives regarding the role of the technology support units was confirmed through interview data with Ethan. Responding to the lack of involvement from technology support in materials development work, Ethan clarified that it wasn't the role of the technology support units to provide such assistance. He stressed the point that the role of such units was to create marketing and digital materials, and they did not support instructors. As for the e-learning unit, their role was to provide professional development training in generalised areas such as how to use video and lecture recording tools. As for the ITS (Information Technology Services) unit, their role was to provide infrastructure support should technical problems such as internet connectivity and equipment malfunctions occur. It was apparent that teachers were unclear on those roles, which led them to question why the technical support units were not involved in materials development work. The efforts of the EAP program to integrate technology were confined to meso-level activities that were not themselves integrated or aligned with broader institutional goals.

The lack of cooperation amongst multi-level stakeholders affects sustainability, as technology integration should be a shared responsibility throughout the institution. Without sufficient support, the burden of responsibility tips too heavily towards teachers, who are often working under time pressure with limited resources. In relation to sustainability, while coping with curricular and technological changes are inevitable aspects of teaching, facing too many of such changes in a non-incremental, unsystematic way (Hinkelman, 2018) can imply that administrators are not aligned with the ongoing needs of teachers.

As we reported earlier, teachers felt that management were not aware of what was happening in the classrooms. In relation to Pillar 4, this sense of disconnect reveals a breakdown in the institution's organisational structures, where the shared roles and responsibilities of technology integration do not seem to align. A quote from Charles illustrates the need for institutional alignment with regard to sustainable technology integration:

> I think at the core of all that has to be some sort of pedagogical basis that . . . this is the model that we're using or these are the theories that are informing what we do, let's all work from the top and bottom to make all of that fit together.
> (Charles, Int. 04, Lines 41.24–41.40)

Little organisational structure was embedded within the change initiatives. As discussed in the beginning of the chapter, Padlet can be likened to a virtual notice board where content structure is determined by the user. The application is unable, for example, to visually organise content based on categories and subcategories like an LMS system. Without an organisational structure embedded into the application, teachers were not able to map the curriculum through Padlet. In turn, such lack of structure made it difficult to transfer macro-level curriculum objectives into micro-level lesson planning. Though not entirely the fault of the application, a lack of structure in the Padlet inhibits the ability to set out a clear curriculum that moves logically from macro- to meso- to micro-level actions. The effect of poor structure is to make the entire curriculum appear to be random and unfocused.

As Charles pointed out in an interview, curriculum planning should ideally begin with an examination of the course objectives and then clearly outline the skills that students need to achieve those objectives. Once these skills have been mapped out, they can be plotted within the program's six thematic modules so that teachers have a macro view of the program in its entirety. Structuring the course content and related materials development work in such a manner would make it easier for teachers working in semi-autonomous groups to identify inconsistencies, prevent overlaps, and ensure a seamless progression of learning materials.

Besides issues with Padlet's lack of structure, the lack of an overall coordinator to structure materials development work affected the outcome of Padlet materials. As noted earlier, the program director, Ethan, fostered an approach of using semi-autonomous groups. Here, teachers were divided into six groups with each group being responsible for one module. This approach was a systematic and efficient way of breaking down the project into more manageable chunks. However, it also undermined efforts to decrease the 'silo' effect that continued to plague program coherence. As each group worked in relative isolation, the lack of inter-group communication and collaboration led to a lack of cohesion in the materials produced. Since curriculum change meant that modules and assessments were inextricably linked, coordination was necessary. Such coordination meant that one or more project groups would need to work in tandem; and at the same time, all groups needed to know what other groups were doing.

With the absence of an overall coordinator, groups of teachers would need to find a time to sit together and share their progress. However, scheduling conflicts among teachers working in different intakes and the need to develop materials as the course progressed did not always make such collaborations feasible. Sophia summarises the lack of collaboration in the semi-autonomous working groups:

> The way we've set it up, again it's not anyone's fault—how else would you do it? But it is very much you guys are doing this and this module and we're still not talking to each other and we're still not recognising build-up.
>
> (Sophia, Int. 04, Lines 7.25–7.37)

As Sophia's account illustrates, the lack of structure in materials development work causes conflicts to arise from interactions between the pillars of environments and tools for learning, and organisational structures. Unsurprisingly, issues with Padlet's lack of structure and the absence of coordinated materials development work were reflected in the resources developed. Interview data revealed that most teachers viewed Padlet resources as a conglomeration of materials as opposed to a well-structured EAP program. Similarly, lessons did not necessarily flow sequentially from one task to the next as reported in the reflective journal entries discussed in Pillar 1. The same lack of cohesion was also confirmed through document analysis of Padlets. At the task level, a close inspection of module tasks showed a lack of cohesion where tasks did not flow seamlessly from one task to the next. At the unit level the lack of progression from one unit to another resulted in the lack of continuous build-up of skills necessary for students to perform in assessments at the end of each module. As was reported with the LMS, there was a similar lack of cohesion among the developed materials, particularly preparatory materials to help students perform in culminating assessments.

To illustrate discrepancies between lesson materials and corresponding assessments, the final module of the program curriculum required students to write a two-sided argumentative essay based on a given prompt. To fulfil the assessment, students would need to read and synthesise the content of two articles, outline their argument, and justify it with supporting details extracted from the given articles. Reflective journal entries describing Cynthia's personal use of the preparatory materials for the argumentative essay assessment revealed inconsistencies in content, organisation, and format in three of the model essays provided. Likewise, field notes of a post-assessment moderation meeting revealed that other teachers voiced similar concerns regarding inconsistencies in the model essays, which could affect the validity of the assessment. However, for a small minority of teachers the variety of formats did not seem to be a matter of concern so long as each teacher adhered to the assessment rubrics.

## Appraising the argument

As set out in the initial phase of the argument, we sought to interrogate the general understanding that "the use of applications is sustainable in language learning programs". As in the previous two case studies, sustainability is viewed in this case study as the 'long-term capacity of socio-cultural and technical systems to exist in ever-evolving educational spaces'. More specifically, we focused on a claim within the context of the case study site of Royal College: 'Padlet will address sustainability issues'. The claim was built on four assumptions: that Padlet would be fit for purpose, used by teachers with minimal training, a means to enhance collegial work, and a way to better structure lesson planning. Considering the data analysis, however, it is arguably a weak claim that the use of Padlet in the Royal College EAP is sustainable.

Briefly, following the structure of the interpretive argument, the domain definition was sound as the assumptions were grounded in the literature. Others have used Padlet in English learning contexts and found the application effective (see Fuchs, 2014; England, 2017; Jacobson, 2015; Lahlafi & Rushton, 2015). The second inference, concerning evaluation of the data collection and its analysis, is also strong: our work meets the demands of longitudinal auto-ethnographic and participatory ethnographic studies, including an ability to blend in with other instructors, take field notes, and involve in constant reflection. The analysis followed the framing set out in Blin et al. (2016) and made use of a wide range of observations.

The third inference involves a need to explain the findings. Insights arising from the analysis begin to show ways in which the use of Padlet is not fully sustainable. To wit, the lack of professional development at the introduction negatively affected the instructors' individual feelings of confidence. Many instructors did not share their work and thus hurt a collegial sense of purpose. The application, though easy to use, was nonetheless insufficient for structuring quality lessons that are required in an academic preparation program. Potentially, the application suits those seeking visual appeal and 'fun' with technology.

Finally, the inference that the application is of utility in Royal College programs is itself weak. During our study, we saw program administrators become less concerned with sustainability in favor of a 'quick fix' that would somehow integrate educational technology and rebuild trust among classroom teachers. One ramification of our findings is that the application is simply unable to meet the academic demands of a university pathways program.

## Summary of the chapter

The purpose of this chapter was to interrogate the sustainability of an application in a blended language program. Initially, the application was introduced to ease the frustrations caused by an earlier attempt to integrate a central LMS: teachers had rejected the system because of its perceived inflexibility and lack of professional development. The application, Padlet, was chosen to address these key issues. Unfortunately, the application was unable to meet the demands inherent in a complex program. Teachers, already shifting work styles and schedules because of increased enrolments, began to develop their own materials that deviated from a standard curriculum. Program leadership did not foster a strong collaborative community that may have better supported the productive use of the application in the classroom. After moving through a series of claims, we concluded that any claim for sustained use was weak. In the next chapter, we summarise the findings of our study and propose an extension to the model of sustainability established by Blin and colleagues (2016). From there, we discuss the implications of our work and suggest an agenda for further research.

## References

Blin, F., Jalkanen, J., & Taalas, P. (2016). Sustainable CALL development. In F. Farr & L. Murray (Eds.), *The Routledge handbook of language learning and technology* (pp. 223–238). Routledge.

Duţă, N., & Martínez-Rivera, O. (2015). Between theory and practice: The importance of ICT in higher education as a tool for collaborative learning. *Procedia—Social and Behavioral Sciences*, *180*, 1466–1473. doi:10.1016/j.sbspro.2015.02.294

England, S. (2017). Tech for the modern EFL student: Collaborate and motivate with Padlet. *Accents Asia*, *9*(2), 56–60.

Fuchs, B. (2014). *The writing is on the wall: Using Padlet for whole-class engagement*. Library and Staff Publications. https://uknowledge.uky.edu/libraries_facpub/240

Graham, M. (2014). Social Media as a tool for increased student participation and engagement outside the classroom in Higher Education. *Journal of Perspectives in Applied Academic Practice*, *2*(3), 16–21.

Gruba, P., Cardenas-Claros, M. S., Suvorov, R., & Rick, K. (2016). *Blended language program evaluation*. Palgrave Macmillan.

Hinkelman, D. (2018). *Blending technologies in second language classrooms*. Palgrave Macmillan.

Jacobson, T. E. (2015). First thoughts on implementing the framework for Information Literacy. *Communications in Information Literacy*, *9*(2), 102.

Lahlafi, A., & Rushton, D. (2015). Engaging international students in academic and information literacy. *New Library World*, *116*(5/6), 277–288. doi:10.1108/NLW-07-2014-0088

Levy, M. (2016). Researching in language learning. In F. Farr & L. Murray (Eds.), *The Routledge handbook of language learning and technology*. Routledge.

Mallon, M., & Bernsten, S. (2015). Collaborative learning technologies. *Tips and Trends Winter 2015, ACRL American Library Association*. Padlet. https://padlet.com

Stockwell, G. (2016). Mobile language learning. In F. Farr, & L. Murray (Eds.), *The Routledge handbook of language learning and technology* (pp. 322–333). Routledge.

van Rooij, S. W. (2009). Adopting open-source software applications in U.S. higher education: A cross-disciplinary review of the literature. *Review of Educational Research*, *79*(2), 682–701. doi:10.3102/0034654308325691

# 5 Towards improved sustainability of technology in blended language programs

Throughout our study, we set out to interrogate the sustainability of blended language learning programs. Drawing concepts from Blin, Jalkanen, and Taalas (2016) into an argument-based approach, we conducted three case studies to examine the integration of a 'device', a 'system', and an 'application'. Qualitative data, including ethnographic observations and interviews, was analysed thematically and the results were then subjected to a formal argumentative process to determine the strength of the claim. In each of the studies, claims of sustainability were seen to be 'weak' and thus sustainable practices were not evident at the site of study.

In this chapter, we discuss our findings to improve the sustainability of technology in blended language learning programs. Ahead of further discussion, we present a summary of our study in Table 5.1

As shown in Table 5.1, we concluded that the integration of technology has not been sustainable at Royal College. Throughout our time at the college, we witnessed a vast number of changes that were often fuelled by the sheer increase in student enrolments. Though technology integration was often at the centre of our discussions and analyses, we were aware that it was not the only element at play within the program: dozens of new staff had to be recruited, on-boarded and settled into offices that, in turn, needed to be furnished and maintained, for example. We saw program administrators work hard as they faced daily challenges, and we worked alongside teachers who put in long hours to help growing numbers of students. Throughout the course of our study, we were privileged to witness a series of fast-paced changes that included ever-increasing student enrolments, new hires, and technology integration that came to dramatically alter many once-familiar ways of working. A study on the impact of change alone could become another large research project; for the moment, we propose our contributions towards theory building, then we move to suggestions for program improvement and set out an agenda for further research.

DOI: 10.4324/b22794-5

*Table 5.1* Summary of case study metaphors

| Metaphor | Research focus | Major findings |
|---|---|---|
| Technology as a device | Sustainability as a pedagogical device (tablet computer) | • The device is unsuitable for pedagogical purposes<br>• The need for internal and external collaboration<br>• The need for targeted professional development training<br>• The need for alignment between top-down and bottom-up perspectives<br>• The need for policy to establish a shared vision of technology integration |
| Technology as a system | Sustainability as a system for capacity building of teachers (LMS) | • Issues in project implementation and administration include power relations and need for clarity in staff roles<br>• The need for teacher professional development |
| Technology as an application | Sustainability as an application for materials development and pedagogy (Padlet) | • Constant changes in curriculum and technology adoption frustrate staff<br>• Misalignment in top-down and bottom-up processes<br>• Need for macro-level awareness of day-to-day realities of EAP classrooms<br>• Need for teacher involvement in macro-level decisions |

## Theory building

The role of technology has never taken a more prominent place in second-language and foreign-language education. Many language teachers and students who had not embraced the use of technology now make use of it daily. Research has begun to emerge on the ramifications caused by this 'emergency remote language teaching,' and more work has yet to be published (Godwin-Jones, 2020). While not wishing to diminish—in any way—the significance of the devasting impact of the pandemic in our field, we maintain a focus on our key question: How can the integration of technology be sustained in blended language programs? Thanks to the pandemic, this question has taken on a greater sense of urgency: without sounding alarmist, our collective ability to make effective use of technology may well be the key factor in the viability of many of our language programs. We think a first step towards greater viability is to build on the work of Blin and colleagues (2016); accordingly, we propose that a fifth pillar be put in place that highlights the need for conceptual insight as a key factor of sustainable program development.

As we worked with data using the four-pillar model of Blin and colleagues (2016), we often encountered material that was not easily captured; that is, quotes from interviews would not fit into existing categories, for example, and aspects of our ethnographic reflections remain unaccounted. In line with Rog (2012), our fifth pillar seeks to recognise the concept of 'contextual insight' to foster in-depth understanding of the circumstances that shape blended environments (Ivanova & Persson, 2017; Chiu, 2018). Bringing forth 'contextual insight' into conceptual framework may help us to consider how the history of a program influences long-term sustainability, as we show in Table 5.2

In our view, cultural change requires the development of a contextual insight that surfaces the history of the program and helps to explain the causes and need for change. According to Schein (2010), culture can be understood as an accepted set of norms, perceptions, and beliefs that have come about through a group's interactions and experiences. Ivanova and

*Table 5.2* Summary of pillar of contextual insight

| Pillar/component | Definition |
|---|---|
| Pillar 5: contextual insight<br>1. Cultural change<br>2. Staff identity<br>3. Emotional impact | Develop an in-depth understanding of the background of a program, idea, or initiative to better anticipate potential areas of sensitivity or growth |
| | Shifts in the way a community functions, interacts, and works with each other |
| | How members of a group perceive and negotiate their place, roles, and responsibilities within their immediate working community, as well as in relation to the wider organisation |
| | The perceived and negotiated place, roles and, responsibilities of group members within their immediate working community and the wider organisation |
| | The perceived achievement of a legitimate status due to factors such as a permanent as opposed to a contract position, and length of service |
| | A strong feeling in response to a situation, personal attitudes, or experiences |

Persson (2017) see changes as an ongoing series of 'transitions' that cultures make as they develop. Synthesising these two points, cultural change can be understood as visible shifts in the way a community functions, interacts, and works. Two elements of cultural change, we think, are particularly important.

In our view, an initial element in understanding and fostering cultural change is to first identify *how it has been already begun* so that appropriate *future* intervention measures can be put in place. At our site of study, Royal College, many changes in the wider institution or its environment had already occurred that influenced sustainable practices. In our longitudinal study, a need for widespread cultural change was set in place because of rapid expansion (Pisapia, Townsend, & Razzaq, 2017) caused by an exponential rise in student numbers. The expansion changed the culture of the blended language program. Starting with a need to provide offices for new staff, administrators necessarily leased new spaces that were distant from one another. No common workspace was available for all staff. Eventually, the dispersion of staff reduced collegiality that, in turn, fragmented program cohesion and continued to worsen as student numbers continued to rise. Engagement frayed.

Without regular opportunities to interact, share information, and collaborate, it may be challenging for staff to adapt to change initiatives (Elliott-Johns, 2015). Based on our knowledge of the organisation's history, relying on 'word of mouth' may have worked when there were small staff numbers and a common shared workspace, but the rapid expansion of the program clearly altered an earlier culture of staff collegiality. For program administrators, an awareness of 'contextual insight' may help to see how changes affect staff collegiality and reduce opportunities for regular engagement that, in turn, harm the sustainability of technology integration.

Secondly, contextual insight recognises the need for a planned institutional change (Ivanova & Persson, 2017) to adapt to extenuating circumstances. Making an argued case for change implies that earlier and necessary (ideal) change has not yet occurred and thus, the desired outcome (which hinges on such change) has not been achieved (Elliott-Johns, 2015). At Royal College, the ideal change (transparency) had not occurred and thus the desired outcome (teacher buy-in) that was vital for change (technology integration) had not been achieved. In other words, fostering transparency is crucial for establishing buy-in when there are major changes planned for the curriculum or technology (Gannaway, Hinton, Berry, & Moore, 2013).

As we completed our analyses, we saw a need to better understand how program staff identities and motives change as they move across institutional levels. Because they engage in multiple roles, for example, program administrators may help to shape directives at the macro level, implement policy at the meso level, and then make use of classroom materials at the micro level (Gruba & Nguyen, 2019). From our bird's-eye analytical view, we witnessed the ways that such fluidity affected sustainable practices; if anything, we thought, key individuals at the meso level needed to highlight the value of their wide understanding of the institution to colleagues at both macro and micro levels. At Royal College, we saw, instructors at the micro level fostered some resistance to changes: could a deeper view of the plans for technology integration be brought on by greater 'contextual insight' of the overall institution? Comparably, staff legitimacy, or the perceived status of instructors because of tenure and length of service, may also require greater acknowledgement. In our observations, staff who felt that their legitimacy was not duly acknowledged resisted the change initiatives. Eventually, we saw how such resistance led to a reduced sense of ownership and harmed the long-term integration of technology.

Emotional impact, or the experience of strong feelings in response to technology integration, can run along a continuum based on personal attitude, perceived institutional support, or sense of motivation (Chiu, 2018). In their study on strategic change in higher education, Pisapia et al. (2017) found that emotions can play a key role in sustaining change. In our analysis, we found that teachers with positive attitudes and experiences with technology were more likely to regard change initiatives as a source of upskilling and the opportunity to develop themselves pedagogically and professionally. On the other hand, teachers with negative experiences may view technology as a source of stress which threatens their views of pedagogical and professional competence. Consequently, the emotional impact of technology integration may lead to technology resistance and affect sustainability. Further, the emotional impact of technology integration can manifest at multiple levels. Being immersed at the site during a period of prolonged instability, we observed how the emotional impact of technology integration intensified as technological and curriculum changes were implemented. As a component of contextual insight, identifying the emotional aspect of technology integration may help to promote sustainability as the negative emotions that staff associate with technology can limit its long-term use and potential for scalability. With a fifth pillar in place, what are the implications of our work that can help to foster sustainable programs?

## Suggestions for improved blended program sustainability

Setting aside the immediate case study of Royal College, we now turn to the implications of our work. In line with the argument-based approach, we hope that our work has utility in that (1) the findings resonate and are powerful enough to stimulate action and (2) our work can be used to identify areas in need of improvement. We seek to align our findings with larger trends, and thus are reminded of the three-tier model of transdisciplinary SLA that was proposed by the Douglas Fir Group (2016). Briefly, the model suggests that language use and acquisition is influenced by aspects of ideology at the macro level, by social institutions at the meso level, and by interactions and activities amongst individuals at the micro level. Gruba, Cardenas-Claros, Suvorov, and Rick (2016) grounded their approach to blended language program evaluation on a similar three-level approach. Significantly, level-based distinctions may help to foster an understanding of the 'complex dynamic systems' that characterise language programs, as such distinctions can help us to better pinpoint our efforts to foster sustainable practices. Table 5.3 presents an example.

We understand that our recommendations are idealised; indeed, to justify such recommendations and foster uptake, further evidence would need to be drawn from document analysis and semi-structured interviews of college leadership. To transfer this argument to another educational context, readers will need to see Royal College as representative of higher education institutions that are well resourced with contemporary educational technologies. Let us try to encourage that transferability.

## *Macro level*

At the macro level, the inability to establish a shared vision of the initiative reduced the emotional investment or 'buy in' from staff. At the meso-level, the perception that technology integration is primarily intended to fulfil policy directives, rather than support learning objectives, may cause teachers to develop a sense of mistrust towards the motivation for change. As emphasised by Pisapia et al. (2017), a misalignment of motivations between program administrators and teachers can lead to resistance towards change initiatives. Further, a perceived lack of institutional support may cause teachers to feel frustration at the sense of disengagement from the upper management, discouraging teachers from playing an effective role as the implementers of technology.

As blending approaches raise our collective expectations of language teachers, we need to draw on Valdés, Kibler, and Walqui (2014) to make visible the four theoretical orientations that underpin language programs; that is, we need to see how a 'theory of language' situates the role of technology in the language classroom and influences our designs for integration. Table 5.4 summarises the four major orientations and their focus on technology.

The concepts shown in Table 5.4 provide much needed groundwork that can help to underpin program management. As we saw over the course of

*Table 5.3* Level-based suggestions for program improvement

| Level of the institution | Motivations for the initial uptake of technology in blended language learning | Factors that diminish sustainable technology integration in blended language programs | Recommendations (idealised) |
|---|---|---|---|
| Macro (ideological structures: belief systems, cultural values, economic values, etc.) | Global enthusiasm; perception of innovation; ease of funding; clear leadership support | Waning global enthusiasm; fewer resourcing considering competing demands; ignoring the need for increased support, replacement, and maintenance | Long-term strategy, policy, and funding arrangements policy; communication across levels; ongoing evaluation reports; recruitment and hiring criteria aligned with blended strategy |
| Meso (sociocultural institutions and communities: social identities, social organisations, etc.) | One-time, dedicated professional development; early positive results of a pilot study; collective use with little resistance | Preferences for a certain teaching style, or choice of device; lack of ongoing professional development; spread of collegial and student dissatisfaction | Collegial mentoring and mutual support; advocacy for keyboards to be provided; sharing resources; collective use and commitment |
| Micro (social activity: semiotic resources) | Novelty and enthusiasm; perception of innovation; single platform; provision of uniform instructions and materials | Lack of keyboard for content creation; diminished enthusiasm; preference for own device; misalignment of utility and tasks on a device | Clear training in pedagogical use of the mobile device; habitual and expected use; device usage integrated in assessment tasks |

our research, three major technology integration projects were launched; no project, however, conducted the necessary planning for their long-term management. Given the need to see how complex interaction of components works together as a single entity (Ison, 2008; Banathy & Jenlink, 2004),

*Table 5.4* Pedagogical orientations to technology integration

| Theoretical orientation | Characteristics and related approaches to teaching | Focal use of technology |
| --- | --- | --- |
| (Early) formal | Language is best learned through memorisation, and competence occurs through alignment with target (native) speakers and writers | Technology helps to present grammatically correct sentences and target patterns of speech that can be imitated |
| Cognitive-interactionist | Language is an ability to use discrete words, utterances, and forms that learners gain through structured practice on their way to fluency | Technology helps learners transition from conscious to automatic thinking through presentation of native patterns of interaction |
| Functional | Language is grounded in a strong awareness of purpose, context, and audience to prepare learners for the specific demands of a field | Technology helps to contextualise the specific context where language is to be used, and provide access to needed forms and materials |
| Sociocultural | Language is situated in dialogic, social interactions that provide learners with the political, conceptual, and interpersonal awareness needed to become competent | Technology is able to present activities to assist learners fas they move from peripheral to central participation |

Source: Based on Valdés et al. (2014, pp. 37–45)

program stakeholders need to foster a greater awareness of common issues, and of one another to reach desired outcomes (Arnold & Wade, 2015). Sustainability is enhanced when there is an alignment of macro-, meso-, and micro-level perspectives of technology integration (Gunn, 2010). Aligned by a shared vision, the various units of an organisation can work synergistically to sustain changes in technology integration. Starting, then, with the macro level, one way forward is to build in organisational behaviour and change management concepts throughout any large-scale change (Schein, 2010) in ways that promote staff ownership (Gill, 2002). Because technology integration may require a wholesale restructure of existing leadership and organisational practices (Brečko, Kampylis, & Punie, 2014), an interdisciplinary perspective of organisational change management (Pisapia et al., 2017) may help sustain the long-term use of technology.

At Royal College, the language program was stable for ten years prior to the introduction of tablet computers in 2012. As we can now see, sudden shifts towards the integration of a technology can affect organisational stability like a 'revolution' (Champoux, 2016). Niemiec and Otte (2009) have long argued the need for institutions to establish the warrants for technology integration ahead of planned program changes. In a related study of macro-level leadership in change management, Schein (2010) identified three key factors that influence success, including, for example, (1) the establishment of a motivation for change, (2) an 'unlearning' and relearning of key concepts, and (3) the need to reinforce areas of targeted change through the reporting and support of positive outcomes. Similarly, Brečko et al. (2014) argued that macro-level leadership needs articulate plans for long-term integration of technology from the very start of announcing their initiatives for change. Indeed, as Champoux (2016) has suggested, leaders need to identify the causes of resistance and manage its effects from the very start of implementing changes in an organisation.

Institutions must invest a significant amount of time to enact a long-term vision of technology integration (Pouezevara, Mekhael, & Darcy, 2014; Fridley & Rogers-Adkinson, 2015). As argued by Elliott-Johns (2015), introducing major curriculum and technology change without a significant investment of time can adversely affect sustainability. Language programs and staff need time necessary to absorb and adapt to change (Littlejohn, 2003; Hinkelman, 2018). Although it may be challenging to establish staff buy-in and build a sense of project ownership (Kennedy & Levy, 2009), program leaders must communicate the rationale for change, set realistic timelines, and map out the pathway to integration. It is important to avoid introducing too many changes that may come to overwhelm staff. As illustrated in our study, decisions to push forward technological and curricular changes at the same time proved to be faulty. Particularly at a time of great increases in student enrolment, teachers did not have time to adjust to a range of changes at the pace set by program leadership.

Given the speed and reach of technological development, decisions that surround resource allocation must consider both current pedagogical demands as well as anticipate future needs. Long-term planning is crucial in such decisions to reduce a temptation to abandon, and wholly replace, educational technology in ways that result in a loss of financial and resource investment. Therefore, a motivating factor for a better understanding of sustainability is to inform sustainable technology adoption and reduce waste stemming from the adoption of systems and approaches that do not meet long-term pedagogical objectives.

Calls for professional development run throughout work in blended language learning (Hinkelman, 2018). Sustainable integration of technology, it is clear, is grounded in the work of teachers who understand technology and its pedagogical applications (Gunn, 2011). Importantly, professional development initiatives should relate technology integration to specific syllabus content, as opposed to surface-level training, which merely covers the typical use of technological applications. As Kennedy and Levy (2009) contend, technical aspects are less important than a focus on the educational value of tools and how to best apply them. Besides training in technology, teachers also need specific training in curriculum development. Such professional development training includes blended lesson design, online materials development, and curriculum and assessment writing. Importantly, professional development initiatives should not be one-off but ongoing, with regular follow-up sessions. Implementing rigorous professional development places significant demands on institutional, financial, and human resources (McGill, Klobas, & Renzi, 2014). As shown in this study and many others, sustainability partially depends on a willingness to invest in the capacity building of teachers. By upskilling teachers and creating more technology 'champions' (Heaton-Shrestha, May, & Burke, 2009), the scalability of technology integration can be further enhanced.

A commitment to sustainable, blended language learning remains a challenge. Administration and program leaders are only too aware of the costs and resources that are needed to maintain the quality of a long-term integration of technology. Language programs do not have much room for budget surplus; to their credit, many institutes favour staff employment ahead of allocation to technology purchases in the face of reduced enrolments and budgets. So, what is the best strategy? If possible, leadership may benefit from seeing technology integration as part of their 'operational' budget and not, for example, as a one-time 'capital' expenditure. That is, akin to the funds allocated each month to pay utilities, for example, we recommend that a modest but ongoing section of budget be dedicated to technology such that the costs become embedded in long-term planning and policy.

At this point, we would like to suggest that language programs adopt a 'principle-based' approach (Patton, 2018b) to underpin their efforts to integrate technology. Although difficult to articulate, principles provide a macro-level basis for decision making. Treating "principles as if they are goals or projects is inappropriate and distorting" (Patton, 2018b, p. 41). We see principles as key to responsibilities of macro-level leaders to set direction and vision. Principles help to express both points of departure and places of destination. For our purposes, a principle-based approach focuses greater attention on institutional processes and recognises the value of community. To surface assumptions and adjust conceptual understandings, principles can start as a series of works in progress or preliminary statements that evolve over time in discussions with program stakeholders. Our own proposed set of example principles for blended language learning program can be found in Table 5.5.

Our proposed principles have evolved through experience over several years. We have adjusted them considering changes in the institutional

*Table 5.5* Example principles for blended language programs

| Value | Principle of the blended language program |
| --- | --- |
| Alignedt | We align our approaches with contemporary concepts of second-language acquisition and related theories in ways that are ethical, inclusive, and just. |
| Collaborative | We work with one another in ways that are respectful, productive, and mutually beneficial. |
| Appropriate | We promote views of technology integration that are sensitive to local technical literacies, cultural practices, and levels of language proficiency. |
| Innovative | We innovate through critical, flexible, and proactive responses to changing environments. |
| Sustainable | We plan so that our program enables long-term, stable, and transferable processes that create meaningful impact. |

*Table 5.6* GUIDE criteria for principles (Patton, 2018a, p. 40) with BLP examples

| GUIDE criteria | BLP example of GUIDE criteria |
| --- | --- |
| Guiding—informs priorities and direction | Fosters a collegial, inclusive approach of technology integration that facilitates teaching, builds capacity, and aligns with larger institutional strategies |
| Useful—informs decisions; feasible | Establishes technology integration through an explicit conceptual framework so that staff and students see value and can justify their efforts |
| Inspiring—values are explicit; basis for long-term engagement | Communicates values in ways that promote an inclusive, sustainable, and engaging approach to technology integration |
| Developmental—sensitive to context and complexity, enduring | Is adaptable, aware, and respectful of pedagogical styles, materials development teams, and institutional norms |
| Evaluable—requires interpretation and judgement of evidence; qualitative with some quantitative results | Use mixed methods to gather evidence to evaluate program principles as a basis for leadership, direction, and sustainability |

strategy as well as in response to feedback from our stakeholders. Significantly, the principles have helped to guide our thinking when the basis for our decision making was murky and unclear, and to this day they are in flux.

To evaluate our principles, we follow the advice of Patton (2018a) to create a survey based on the GUIDE criteria (Table 5.6). Through the instrument, we ask our stakeholders how they perceive the program leadership team demonstrates its commitment to principles as shown in the ways they set priorities, inform decisions, and inspire staff. Results of the survey help our program leadership adjust actions and respond to key stakeholders.

In addition to setting principles, macro-level leaders can benefit from improved planning. Fairly well known throughout the social sciences, concepts in the 'theory of change' literature may be useful in our efforts to sustain technology integration in our blended language programs. Originally coined by Weiss (1995), a theory of change helps to articulate the mini-steps needed to foster change; it is important to note that those steps should take place *during the planning process* to anticipate where issues may arise. For those unfamiliar with the concept, an online search of the term reveals a range of sources that include a summary by Montague-Clouse and Taplin (2011) and brief explanation by van der Laan (2019). Briefly, working on a theory of change does not entail crafting how change may happen but turns attention to the importance of setting out detailed planning processes that are specific to a program. After establishing what they would like to accomplish, such as the adoption of Padlet, program leaders and language instructors would come together to discuss how an initiative will unfold. Starting from a step-by-step backwards process of mapping, participants set out all the necessary pre-conditions that are required for success (Montague-Clouse & Taplin, 2011). Crucially, such a structured process of thinking helps to surface many of the assumptions that each of us may hold as we consider a change. Our work on the 'argument-based' approach leads us towards a comparable way of thinking: what are the warrants, assumptions, and claims that underpin our efforts? Drawing concepts from work in the theory of change, implementation science, and related fields of change management would strengthen our own contribution to increase the use of argument-based approaches now popular in applied linguistics. To illustrate, Table 5.7 sets out questions and statements that have helped us to foster theory of change with our colleagues.

Even as they work out plans plan through a theory of change, macro-level leaders may like to make use of the capacity maturity model (CMM) as a means to inform their progress towards sustainability. First used in the field of software engineering, modified forms of CMM have been applied to areas from business management to corporate training through to self-help advice to assess progress towards sustainable practices (Wagenstein, 2006). We provide a summary of the classic five stages in Table 5.8.

From experience, implementing some form of a CMM based on concepts shown in Table 5.8 may help staff assess progress. Though an argument-based evaluation may provide programs with an appraisal of the strength of claims, for example, such analysis fails to track the stages of program

*Table 5.7* Example theory of change prompts for discussion

| Question for discussion | Preliminary statement |
| --- | --- |
| What is it: define the task | Blended Language Program (BLP) materials incorporaten the design, production, and publication of resources that foster the uptake of policy by researchers who use the materials to understand and enact their responsibilities |
| How crucial is it: establish the warrant | The BLP project is the basis for enacting the Technology Integration Policy set by institution leadership in February 2020. |
| Who is best for it: write a position description | A person with experience in BLP, organisational leadership, and team-driven materials writing; the position requires specialised knowledge and an ability to direct materials development teams who hold a range of graduate degrees |
| How is it evaluated: set out the expectations for success | BLP uptake will succeed when researchers undertake their responsibilities; materials help to motivate and guide researcher actions; the outputs will be presented in a summary report in July 2022. |
| When will it run: create a schedule for the project | Materials will need to accompany the roll-out of the BLP project from September 2021; project is set to conclude after a full review of the program in September 2022. |

*Table 5.8* Summary of a five-stage CMM model

| Stage | Description |
| --- | --- |
| 1. Initial | As procedures in this stage have not been systematised, they are characterised as being 'reactive' and lacking clearly established guidelines, making subsequent replication in future projects difficult. Individual heroics' bring positive outcomes but often mask the need to better establish systems. |
| 2. Repeatable/ managed | In this stage, key procedures have been put in place and formalised, making possible subsequent replication in future projects. However, these procedures are applied to isolated projects, and are often still considered 'reactive'. |
| 3. Defined | At this stage, the organisation aspires to streamline systems for the management and documentation of isolated projects. While being more organised, projects are mainly 'siloed'. |
| 4. Predictable | At this stage, organisational procedures and systems are applied and streamlined across departments. Achievement of organisational goals is formalised rather than unpredictable. |
| 5. Optimising | At this stage, the concern is ongoing refinement of existing procedures and the capacity to adapt to the changing circumstances of the organisation. |

Source: Adapted from Wagenstein (2006)

development. Institutional discussions that may surround the definition and adoption of a local version of a maturity model are well worth the effort. For those at the macro level, developing a sense of progress may help to place, expand, or contract limited resources. Program stakeholders further afield, including potential funders, may show an interest. Further down, at the meso level, indicators of progress may help to make visible the widespread efforts that are required to instantiate technology integration and thus provide some motivation for continuation. At the micro level, teachers and students can gain a sense of how their own efforts contribute to the larger initiative.

## *Meso level*

At the meso level, program administrators can foster clarity of staff identity by outlining straightforward reporting structures and ensuring that technological change is implemented incrementally and systematically (Hinkelman, 2018). As Gunn (2010) advises, clear guidelines promote a shared understanding of technology integration and build staff accountability. By extension, clear policies regarding technology adoption can also clarify the role of staff in achieving that shared vision.

As key drivers of sustainability, explicating the rationale for change, implementing a realistic timeline, and setting out clear processes for its execution are also crucial to encourage project ownership (Kennedy & Levy, 2009). A way to build staff ownership is to acknowledge the role of legitimacy and involve senior staff such as teachers in the pre-planning and development stages of curriculum and technology change, so that they are more likely to be invested throughout the process of development and long-term adoption. If senior staff regard not being consulted as a lack of acknowledgement and a threat to their legitimacy, then they may react by showing resistance (Gill, 2002) towards any efforts for technology and curriculum change. Should such resistance not be addressed, however, a negative departmental culture can fester to the point where staff may come to see change initiatives as unwarranted and thus not worth the effort (Gruba et al., 2016). It is crucial to build staff ownership from the initial stages of project planning through an explicit recognition of the potential wealth of contextual insights of senior staff.

Program sustainability can be achieved by integrating the time and effort needed for the reflection, review, and redevelopment of blended learning projects (Kennedy & Levy, 2009). Such iterative processes can be conducted through a review meeting to evaluate the strengths, weaknesses, and areas of improvement at the end of each teaching cycle. Based on feedback, program improvement (Norris, 2016) can inform the next cycle of teaching.

Investing time for such processes is crucial to refine a program, though it may entail investment over a period of no less than two to three years (Patton, 2011). Importantly, sustainability entails being flexible to changing circumstances—namely, when curriculum and technological change requires more time than originally anticipated. In such cases, priority should be given to improving existing curriculum and resources instead of conducting a complete overhaul when the expected change is not achieved. Through a tripartite process that involves reflection, review, and redevelopment, a blended language learning program stands a much greater chance of becoming mature enough to meet a long-term vision of change.

Another pedagogical implication for sustainability is the importance of creating opportunities for collaboration. The first type of collaboration entails creating and sustaining a community of practice for teachers (Kennedy & Levy, 2009). As we have discussed, meeting the pressing needs of a rapidly expanding student population led to the fragmentation of staff cohesion, as shown in dispersed workspace locations and conflicting timetables. Such fragmentation limited the opportunities to discuss teaching experiences and share resources. To foster mutual support, we suggest scheduling regular events to provide teachers with the opportunity to voice their concerns and share their experiences of technology integration. To encourage the scalability of resources, such meetings should allow teachers to present resources and encourage others to build on the work of colleagues.Both institutional and mutual support may help teachers negotiate the changes that are inherent in the widespread adoption of blended approaches.

In line with the establishment of a broader 'theory of change' at the macro level, we suggest that meso-level program leaders enact a series of mini-steps that identify what is to be done, its underlying assumptions, and the expected result of the action. A search for 'theory of change' templates may help find material (e.g., diytoolkit.org/tools/theory-of-change/); in Table 5.9, we set out an example of our recent work to illustrate ways we have begun to implement such processes.

As we saw, the quality of program leadership at the meso level was a key element of technology integration at Royal College; at times, as detached researchers, we felt it could have been improved. Upon reflection, though, we asked: where would language instructors get leadership training? In our own programs, it is often the 'most experienced' or perhaps 'most ambitious' staff member who either volunteers or is selected to lead a major initiative. As CALL and blended learning professionals, how can we help one another improve our leadership capabilities? One often cited definition of leadership is "the process of interpersonal influence in which direct and indirect means are employed to get others to accomplish the organization's goals, where influence is achieved by providing purpose, direction, and

Towards improved sustainability 103

Table 5.9 Suggested areas to enact a theory of change

| Activity | Assumption | Output | Notes |
|---|---|---|---|
| Appoint a BLP materials lead | The appointee knows what is required and has the skills and authority to do the work | Position description | Someone external to the present BLP group? |
| Create a communications plan | The communications plan is sufficient to cover the campus in a logical and defensible manner | Communications plan | Resources are available? |
| Work with specialists to create materials | The lead can transform the comms plan into actual materials through work with a small team | A suite of materials is created | Can we recruit learning materials specialists from other areas of the college? |
| The materials are accurate, appropriate, and published | The materials are published in media and locations that researchers can find | List of sites | Do the materials need to appear in multiple locations? |
| The materials are used by researchers | The materials are fit for purpose and easily found by researchers | Tracking downloads | Are descriptive statistics sufficient, or are user interviews needed? |
| The materials require updating and revision | Revision and updating are easy | Revision logs | Short-term revisions are needed frequently but made by original team? |
| The materials are fit for purpose over the long term, including substantial revision efforts | Research input about the materials has been gathered and integrated in revised designs | Revision logs/actual materials | Sufficient information has been transmitted to a new team who understand the materials |
| Materials are maintained | Responsibility for long-term maintenance has been determined | Clear statement of responsibility created | Resources are available and allocated |

motivation" (Schunn, McGregor, & Saner, 2005, p. 1379). Ideally, strong leaders handle complex day-to-day issues, work across organisational levels, and promote the need to adopt a nuanced understanding of the fluid intersections of pedagogy, policy, and technology. In summary, we recommend that program leaders gain a keen sense of what leadership requires, make clear their short and long-term plans for technology integration, and help foster staff efforts to collaborate and support one another as they undertake blended approaches to language learning.

## *Micro level*

Pedagogical practices at the micro level also influence sustainability. When harnessed effectively, technology enables various affordances which can transform classroom experiences (Healey, 2016). These affordances can be hindered, however, if technology is not used in a thoughtful, systematic, and planned way (Selwyn, 2013; Hinkelman, 2018). More specifically, teachers question the underlying motives of technology integration if they suspect such motives to place commercial, marketing, and cost-effectiveness needs above teaching and learning. It is a recurring theme in this study that the motivation for technology use is weakened if teachers distance themselves from technology and do not perceive it as adding any pedagogical value (Gruba & Nguyen, 2019). Therefore, starting from the planning stages, the adoption of technology must align with pedagogical goals and styles. In other words, the integration of technology must be appropriate to the context of the curriculum and serve the needs of pedagogy, rather than the other way around. One way forward is to ensure that teachers have greater involvement in the choice of tools and designs of their courses (Gunn, 2011). By considering teachers' input, a blended curriculum is more likely to benefit students by being highly localised, learner-centred, and driven by authentic learning experiences (Eskildsen & Theodórsdóttir, 2015).

Perhaps initially unforeseen, work with "new technologies make[s] visible aspects of the pedagogic practice that were previously taken for granted" (Beetham & Sharpe, 2007, p. 7). This can unsettle teachers. As a way to prepare, Garrett (2009) suggests that language educators think about a key question:

> What kind of software [I would now substitute "technology-based learning activities"], integrated how, into what kind of syllabus, at what level of language learning, for what kind of language learners, is likely to be effective for what specific learning purposes?
>
> (p. 721)

As we have seen throughout this study, teachers see that blended technology is effective only when embedded in the curriculum. Teachers also highlighted the oft-repeated point that ongoing professional development that involves both technological and pedagogical support is the only means to sustain blended approaches (Chambers & Bax, 2006). Starting from the macro level, effective blending takes place when program administrators encourage, and indeed come to expect, that technology be integrated throughout the institution (Hinkelman, 2018); with that expectation, teachers at the micro level can proceed with confidence, knowing that their work is supported and recognised.

Arguably, the bulk of CALL and related blended language learning research has concerned the micro level (see, for example, Healey, 2016), grounded in cognitive linguistics, psycholinguistics, human learning, and language in social context (Chapelle, 2009). Here, we urge more research to inform ways that micro-level activities consider the immediate social context of the organisation. From our close interaction at the micro level, ensuring that teachers have an understanding the organisation's vision of technology integration helps them to better align their pedagogical approaches to that shared vision. Even as macro and meso leaders set out such views, however, we see a need to bolster instructor willingness to engage with the processes of strategy and planning. How can staff at the micro level, often pressed to both develop materials and teach classes, better engage with the two upper levels of an organisation?

## Suggestions for further research

Our views of blended language learning are rapidly changing, and the metaphors of technology we have used to reach the "full integration of technology, theory, and pedagogy" (Garrett, 2009) are now being seen as part of a larger 'porous classroom' that has the potential to blur earlier divisions between our places, configurations, or the roles to foster "a vision for inclusive, engaged, and transformative language learning" (Godwin-Jones, 2020, p. 10). As our pedagogical activities at the micro level flow through to the meso-level social institutions of our organisations and raise awareness of the macro level of ideology, Godwin-Jones hopes, porosity in our teaching may well help to improve social cohesion and the acceptance of others.

Part of our emerging research in porosity must involve graduate student training; that is, we need empirical support as we begin to refocus our attention to what is taught in CALL teacher education programs to align with new concepts of language and interaction. Some of that training must now include attention to the value of long-term planning, ongoing budget allocation, and continued professional development. In our crowded curriculum, where do we make space for the serious discussion of blended program administration? Perhaps the growing adoption of the three-level view of SLA (The Douglas Fir Group, 2016) may heighten the value of discussing concepts of sustainable integration. It is at the meso level where teachers discuss the curriculum, align lessons and assessments, and seek to make the student experience coherent. Awareness, as simple as asking one another about the day's lessons, is fostered by regular informal conversations as well as through regular staff meetings. Such research would help to build a stronger conceptual foundation for professional development in language program leadership. With greater recognition and development, language professionals themselves could better see that leadership is a strong factor in sustaining programs, conserving resources, and enhancing the overall quality of student learning.

The Douglas Fir Group (2016) offer us an opportunity, too, to take our research into ways that better recognise the importance of ideology and social institutions as we situate our blended programs in university departments, schools, and other large organizations and institutions. Though it is understandable that micro-level considerations have been a major focus of CALL and blended language learning, we need to encourage more investigation at the meso and macro levels of technology-enhanced language learning (Godwin-Jones, 2020); that is, we need to encourage greater attention to the departmental, institutional, and national factors that influence technology use. Fortunately, with the backing of SLA experts and their three-tier model (Douglas Fir Group, 2016), we now have a collective license to conduct research that goes beyond our earlier techno-centric views of technology-based acquisition that have, to date, focused on individual student or small group interactions with computers. Following a review of the nature of complex multi-level interactions, it would be insightful to first plan, and then track, why particular decisions are made, how they are enacted and where tensions occur. The field would benefit through a greater understanding of the basis for decision making in blended language learning, and how key interventions may act to promote greater pedagogical and technological alignment.

Other studies of alignment, we think, could investigate the ramifications of fluid professional roles and identity in language programs (Gruba & Nguyen, 2019). As they take on various institutional responsibilities, institutional staff move across organisational levels from upper administration to classroom teaching. Thus, a study on alignment could explore the complexities of negotiating among such organisational levels and reconciling the inevitable tensions that stakeholders face as they navigate various roles. To illustrate, such a study could illuminate how program administrators at the meso level function and the role that alignment can play in making more informed decisions regarding curricular and technological change initiatives. Additionally, class observations focusing on how lesson materials are translated into the classroom could determine the extent that blended learning approaches align with broader institutional goals.

Over the past five years, our research has focused on sustainability, but since that time the world has changed: the pandemic has affected every aspect of our professional lives and has deeply hurt the area of language teaching and learning. Royal College, the site of our study, is now struggling to maintain the language program. Many other language programs and universities have lost much, too, and it is now clear that the sustainability of our teaching, classrooms, and uses of technology has taken on an ever-increasing prominence.

## References

Arnold, R. D., & Wade, J. P. (2015). A definition of systems thinking: A systems approach. *Procedia Computer Science*, *44*, 669–678. doi:10.1016/j.procs.2015.03.050

Banathy, B. H., & Jenlink, P. M. (2004). Systems inquiry and its application in education. In D. H. Jonassen (Ed.), *Handbook of research on educational communications and technology* (2nd ed., pp. 37–57). Lawrence Erlbaum.

Beetham, H., & Sharpe, R. (2007). An introduction to rethinking pedagogy for a digital age. In H. Beetham & R. Sharpe (Eds.), *Rethinking pedagogy for a digital age* (pp. 1–10). Routledge.

Blin, F., Jalkanen, J., & Taalas, P. (2016). Sustainable CALL development. In F. Farr & L. Murray (Eds.), *The Routledge handbook of language learning and technology* (pp. 223–238). Routledge.

Brečko, B. N., Kampylis, P., & Punie, Y. (2014). *Mainstreaming ICT-enabled innovation in education and training in Europe: Policy actions for sustainability, scalability, and impact at system level*. Publications Office of the European Union. https://publications.jrc.ec.europa.eu/repository/handle/JRC83502

Chambers, A., & Bax, S. (2006). Making CALL work: Towards normalisation. *System*, *34*, 465–479.

Champoux, J. E. (2016). *Organizational behavior: Integrating individuals, groups, and organizations*. Routledge.

Chapelle, C. A. (2009). The relationship between second language acquisition theory and computer-assisted language learning. *The Modern Language Journal*, *93*, 741–753. doi:10.1111/j.1540-4781.2009.00970.x

Chiu, H. H. (2018). Employees' intrinsic and extrinsic motivations in innovation implementation: The moderation role of managers' persuasive and assertive strategies. *Journal of Change Management*, *18*(3), 218–239. doi:10.1080/14697017.2017.1407353

Douglas Fir Group, T. (2016). A transdisciplinary framework for SLA in a multilingual world. *The Modern Language Journal*, *100*, 19–47.

Elliott-Johns, S. E. (2015). Leadership for change in contemporary teacher education. In S. E. Elliott-Johns (Ed.), *Leadership for change in teacher education: Voices of Canadian deans of education* (pp. 1–6). SensePublishers.

Eskildsen, S. W., & Theodórsdóttir, G. (2015). Constructing L2 learning spaces: Ways to achieve learning inside and outside the classroom. *Applied Linguistics*, 38(2), 143–165. doi:10.1093/applin/amv010

Fridley, D., & Rogers-Adkinson, D. (2015). Implementing a one-to-one technology Initiative in Higher Education. *Administrative Issues Journal: Connecting Education, Practice, and Research*, 5(2), 38–50.

Gannaway, D., Hinton, T., Berry, B., & Moore, K. (2013). Cultivating change: Disseminating innovation in higher education teaching and learning. *Innovations in Education and Teaching International*, 50(4), 410–421.

Garrett, N. (2009). Computer-Assisted Language Learning trends and issues revisited: Integrating innovation. *The Modern Language Journal*, 93, 719–740. doi:10.1111/j.1540-4781.2009.00969.x

Gill, R. (2002). Change management—or change leadership? *Journal of Change Management*, 3(4), 307–318. doi:10.1080/714023845

Godwin-Jones, R. (2020). Building the porous classroom: An expanded model for blended language learning. *Language Learning & Technology*, 24(3), 1–18.

Gruba, P., Cardenas-Claros, M. S., Suvorov, R., & Rick, K. (2016). *Blended language program evaluation*. Palgrave Macmillan.

Gruba, P., & Nguyen, N. B. C. (2019). Evaluating technology integration in a Vietnamese university language program. *Computer Assisted Language Learning*, 32(5–6), 619–637.

Gunn, C. (2010). Sustainability factors for e-learning initiatives. *ALT-J: Research in Learning Technology*, 18(2), 89–103. doi:10.1080/09687769.2010.492848

Gunn, C. (2011). Sustaining eLearning innovations. In G. Williams, P. Statham, N. Brown, & B. Cleland (Eds.), *Changing demands, changing directions: Proceedings ascilite Hobart 2011* (pp. 509–519). www.ascilite.org.au/conferences/hobart11/procs/Gunn-full.pdf

Healey, D. (2016). Language learning and technology past, present and future. In F. Farr & L. Murray (Eds.), *The Routledge handbook of language learning and technology*. Routledge.

Heaton-Shrestha, C., May, S., & Burke, L. (2009). Student retention in higher education: What role for virtual learning environments? *Journal of Further and Higher Education*, 33, 83–92. doi:10.1080/03098770802645189

Hinkelman, D. (2018). *Blending technologies in second language classrooms*. Palgrave Macmillan.

Ison, R. (2008). Systems thinking and practice for action research. In P. Reason & H. Bradbury (Eds.), *The SAGE handbook of action research: Participative inquiry and practice* (pp. 139–158). Sage.

Ivanova, O., & Persson, S. (2017). Transition as a ubiquitous and a continuous process: Overcoming the Western view. *Journal of Change Management*, 17(1), 31–46. doi:10.1080/14697017.2016.1185643

Kennedy, C., & Levy, M. (2009). Sustainability and computer-assisted language learning: Factors for success in a context of change. *Computer Assisted Language Learning*, 22(5), 445–463.

Littlejohn, A. (2003). Supporting sustainable e-learning. *Association for Learning Technology Journal, 11*(3), 88–102.

McGill, T. J., Klobas, J. E., & Renzi, S. (2014). Critical success factors for the continuation of e-learning initiatives. *The Internet and Higher Education, 22*, 24–36.

Montague-Clouse, L., & Taplin, D. (2011). Theory of change basics. *ActKnowledge*. theoryofchange.org/wp-content/uploads/toco_library/pdf/2011_-_Montague-Clouse_-_Theory_of_Change_Basics.pdf

Niemiec, M., & Otte, G. (2009). An administrator's guide to the whys and hows of blended learning. *Journal of Asynchronous Learning Networks, 13*(1), 19–30.

Norris, J. M. (2016). Language program evaluation. *The Modern Language Journal, 100*(S1), 169–189. doi:10.1111/modl.12307

Patton, M. Q. (2011). *Developmental evaluation: Applying complexity concepts to enhance innovation and use*. The Guilford Press.

Patton, M. Q. (2018a). *Principles-focused evaluation: The GUIDE*. Sage.

Patton, M. Q. (2018b). A historical perspective on the evolution of evaluative thinking. In A. T. Vo & T. Archibald (Eds.), *Evaluative thinking. New Directions for Evaluation, 158*, 11–28.

Pisapia, J., Townsend, T., & Razzaq, J. (2017). Strategic change in the academy: Controlling and/or enabling strategies. *Journal of Change Management, 17*(4), 321–343. doi:10.1080/14697017.2016.1253601

Pouezevara, S., Mekhael, S. W., & Darcy, N. (2014). Planning and evaluating ICT in education programs using the four dimensions of sustainability: A program evaluation from Egypt. *International Journal of Education and Development Using Information and Communication Technology, 10*(2), 120–141.

Rog, D. J. (2012). When background becomes foreground: Toward context-sensitive evaluation practice. *New Directions for Evaluation, 2012*(135), 25–40.

Schein, E. H. (2010). *Organizational culture and leadership*. Wiley.

Schunn, C., McGregor, M. U., & Saner, L. D. (2005). Expertise in ill-defined problem-solving domains as effective strategy use. *Memory & Cognition, 33*(8), 1377–1387.

Selwyn, N. (2013). *Distrusting educational technology: Critical questions for changing times*. Routledge.

Valdés, G., Kibler, A., & Walqui, A. (2014). *Changes in the expertise of ESL professionals: Knowledge and action in an era of new standards*. www.tesol.org/docs/default-source/papers-and-briefs/professional-paper-26-march-2014.pdf?sfvrsn=2

van der Laan, A. (2019). *How to design a Theory of Change* (blog). Akvo, Amsterdam. Retrieved June 2021 from datajourney.akvo.org/blog/how-to-design-a-theory-of-change

Wagenstein, H. N. (2006). *A capability maturity model for training & education*. Chapter One: Background and rationale. Project Management Institute. www.pmi.org/learning/library/capability-maturity-model-training-education-8102

Weiss, C. (1995). Nothing as practical as good theory: Exploring theory-based evaluation for Comprehensive Community Initiatives for children and families. In J. P. Connell, A. C. Kubisch, L. B. Schorr, & C. H. Weiss (Eds.), *New approaches to evaluating community initiatives* (pp. 65–92). Aspen Institute.

# Author Index

Agar, J. xi
Agostinho, S. 1, 48
Ahmed, K. 23, 24
Anderson, H. xiii
Arnold, R. D. 38, 95
Australian Government, Federal Register of Legislation 44

Banathy, B. H. 35, 37, 38, 94
Barr, D. x, xiii
Barret, B. xiii
Beetham, H. 104
Bennett, S. 1, 2, 7, 8, 9, 58
Berardino, L. xiii
Bernsten, S. 64
Berry, B. 8, 91
Bishop, L. 16
Blin, F. 9, 10, 11, 15, 17, 18, 34, 35, 43, 44, 47, 58, 62, 70, 77, 81, 86, 87, 88, 90
Bodily, R. G. xii, 34
Borowy, I. 1
Bowen, G. A 15
Bowles, A. R. 13, 57
Brečko, B. N. 11, 47, 95, 96
Brundtland, G. H. 1

Cardenas-Claros, M. S. xiv, 5, 42, 66, 93
Carrasco, B. xiii
Cerone, A. 1
Chambers, A. 105
Champoux, J. E. xii, 96
Chapelle, C. 10, 11, 12, 13, 18, 105
Chen Hsieh, J. S. 44
Chiu, H. H. 90, 92

Crookes, G. xii, 38
Cuban, L. ix, 2, 3, 4, 5

Darcy, N. 6, 96
Demirkan, H. 37
De Wever, B. 15
Donanci, S. xiii, 35
Douglas Fir Group, T. xv, 13, 93, 106
Duţă, N. 64
Dyson, L. E. xiii, 29

Edwards, S. L. xiii, 40
Egbert, J. xii
Elliott-Johns, S. E. 91, 96
Engin, M. xiii, 35, 91, 96, 99
England, S. 62, 63, 64, 86
Enright, M. K. 11
Eskildsen, S. W. 10

Farr, F. xii
Frank, V. M. 13, 57
Freynik, S. 13, 34, 57
Fridley, D. 5, 8, 9, 96
Fuchs, B. 62, 63, 64, 71, 86

Gannaway, D. 8, 9, 11
Garrett, N. xiv, 104, 105
Garrison, R. xiii
Geva, S. xiii, 40
Gill, R. 101
Gimeno Sanz, A. M. x, 2
Gleason, J. xiii, xiv, 12
Godwin-Jones, R. xiv, 89, 105, 106
Golonka, E. M. 13, 57
Graham, C. R. xii, xiii, 34, 63
Green, D. xiii, 29

Grgurovic, M. xiii
Gruba, P. ix, x, xi, xiii, xiv, xv, 5, 8, 9, 10, 13, 14, 18, 26, 39, 42, 58, 66, 67, 92, 93, 101, 104, 106
Grunberg, J. xii
Gunn, C. xi, xii, 8, 9, 10, 95, 96, 101, 104

Hall, G. 7, 8, 9
Hardaker, G. 5, 48
Harrison, J. B. xiii
Healey, D. xiii, 10, 104, 105
Heaton-Shrestha, C. 51, 97
Hinkelman, D. x, xi, xii, xiii, 10, 37, 39, 40, 46, 62, 83, 96, 104, 105
Hinton, T. 8, 91
Hocky, N. xii
Hooey, C. 1
Howard, S. K. xiii, 5, 6, 7, 8, 9
Hubbard, P. xiii, 10

Ison, R. 94
Ivanova, O. 90, 91

Jacobson, T. 62, 63, 64, 86
Jalkanen, J. x, 10, 27, 70, 88
Jamieson, J. M 11
Jenlink, P. M. 35, 37, 38, 94
Jenson, J. xii, 12
Johnson, S. M. xiii, 23
Jones, D. P. 1, 8, 9
Jones, K. A. xii, xiii

Kampylis, P. 11, 47, 95
Kane, M. 11
Kern, R. xi
Kibler, A. 93
Klobas, J. E. 6, 47, 97
Kress, G. 17
Kubanyiova, M. xii, 38

Lahlafi, A. 63, 86
Lee, T. 11, 13
Levy, M. x, xiii, 10, 11, 31, 51, 62, 96, 97, 101, 102
Littlejohn, A. x, 1, 10, 96
Lockyer, L. 1, 48
Lotherington, H. xii, 12
Lynch, B. K. 15

MacDonald, J. D. xii
Mallon, M. 64
Marek, M. W. 44
Margaryan, A. 1
Martínez-Rivera, O. 64
Mason, A. 1
McCarthy, M. xiii
McDonald, P. xii, 1, 2
McGill, T. J 6, 47, 97
McGregor, M. U. 104
Mekhael, S. W. 6, 96
Mele, C. 37
Merriam, S. B. xiv
Mizza, D. xiii
Montague-Clouse, L. 99
Moore, K. 8, 91
Murphy, L. xiii
Murray, L. xii

Naidoo, E. xiii, 29
Nasser, O. 23, 24
Neumeier, P. xiii
Nicolson, M. xiii
Niederhauser, D. S. 5, 6, 7, 8, 9
Niemiec, M. 96
Norris, J. M. xiv, 101
Nworie, J. x, 1, 7, 8
Nykvist, S. xiii, 40

Oliver, M. xiii
Olminkhof, C. xiii, 29
Otte, G. 96
Owen, G. T. 15
Owston, R. xi

Patton, M. Q. ix, xiv, 15, 17, 37, 38, 97, 98, 102
Pels, J. 37
Persson, S. 90, 91
Pisapia, J. 91, 92, 95
Polese, F. 37
Porter, W. W. xiii, 34
Pouezevara, S. 6, 7, 96
Punie, Y. 11, 47, 95

Rabidoux, S. 44
Ragnedda, M. xii
Raji, M. 7, 8, 9
Razzaq, J. 91
Renzi, S. 6, 47, 97

Richardson, D. L 13, 57
Rick, K. xiv, 5, 14, 42, 66, 93
Robertson, I. 10
Rog, D. J. 90
Rogers-Adkinson, D. 5, 8, 9, 96
Rottmann, A. 44
Rubio, F. xiii
Rushton, D. 63, 86

Sandberg, D. S. xii, 34
Saner, L. D. 104
Sayago, S. 15
Schalock, R. L. 11
Schein, E. H. 90, 95, 96
Schellens, T. 15
Schmandt, J. x
Scholz, K. W. 6, 39
Schulze, M. 6, 39
Schunn, C. 104
Selwyn, N. 58, 104
Sharma, R. S. xii, xiii
Sharpe, R. 104
Singh, G. 5, 48
Somekh, B. xiv
Southgate, M. xiii
Spector, J. M. 7
Statista xii
Stein, J. xiii
Stepanyan, K. x, 1, 2, 5
Stern, D. M. 2, 39, 40, 49
Summers, M. xii
Suvorov, R. xiv, 5, 42, 66, 93

Taalas, P. x, 10, 29, 70, 88
Taplin, D. 99
Tatum, B. D. 1
Theodórsdóttir, G. 10, 104
Thorne, K. xiii
Timmis, S. 1, 8, 9
Toh, Y. 2, 5, 6, 8, 9
Townsend, T. 91
Trigwell, K. xiii
Triplett, J. 1

Valcke, M. 15
Valdés, G. 93, 96
van der Laan, A. 99
Van Keer, H. 15
van Rooij, S. 62
Vaughan, H. xiii
Verdugo, M. 11
Voogt, J. xiii, 5, 6, 7, 8, 9

Wade, J. P. 38, 95
Wagenstein, H. 99, 100
Walqui, A. 93
Waters, A. xi, xii, 15
Weiss, C. 99
Welker, J. xiii
Wen-Chi Wu, V. 44
Willits, M. D. D. xiii, 2, 39, 40, 49
Woodfield, W. xiii

Yin, R. K. 15

Zanjani, N. xiii, 40
Zualkernan, I. 8, 9

# Subject Index

academic literacy 63
action research 66–67
affordance 7, 10, 43, 64, 104
alignment 68–72, 89, 106–107
Android 29–30
appraisal 13, 34, 99
appraising the argument viii, 13, 23, 33, 56, 85
appropriateness 33, 68–72
argument-based xv, 12–14, 18, 33, 56, 88, 99
assumption 14, 27, 34, 56–57, 85, 97–99, 102

blended language learning 13–17, 26–27, 37–44, 56–59, 65, 86–94, 106–107
BOCR (benefits, opportunities, resources, and risks) 9
bottom-up 40, 79, 89

capacity building 41–47, 57, 79, 97
case study 34–42, 57–59, 65–66, 85
claim 12–14, 23–26, 34–35, 41–43, 56–58, 85–86
Clickview 25
community and knowledge building xv, 31–32, 49–50, 79–81
complex adaptive systems 6, 38–39
computer-assisted language learning (CALL) 10–11, 102–106
consistency 24, 68
curriculum xii, 50, 79–85, 97, 102–106

dimensions of sustainability 6–7
document analysis 15, 33, 44, 47, 70, 85, 93

domain definition 13, 25–27, 33–34, 56–57, 66, 86

EAP (English for Academic Purposes) xiv, 13, 17, 25–32, 50–52, 65–67, 77–83
environments and tools for learning xiv–xv, 27, 35, 44, 70
ethics xiv, 13, 25
ethnographic 33, 44, 57, 66–68, 88–90

face-to-face xiii, 13, 25–27, 45–46, 63–64
feedback 7, 38, 53, 80, 98
field notes 28–29, 44, 57–58, 68–70, 75–80, 85–86
flipped 25, 44–46, 64

Good Reader 25
Google 25, 28, 77, 80

inference 13–14, 33–34, 57, 86
innovation 1–7, 15, 18, 38, 48
interpretive arguments 11–15, 25–27, 35, 42, 56–58, 86
interviews 16–17, 25–29, 32–33, 43–46, 74, 90–93
iPad 23–24, 29, 33

keyboard 29

leadership 11, 15, 34–35, 56–59, 68, 74–75, 86, 95–100
learning objectives 27, 68, 93

macro level xv, 13, 33–35, 58, 67, 80–84, 93–97, 101–105

## 114 *Subject Index*

materials development 2, 24–25, 30, 39, 66–71, 79–86
meso level 13–15, 25, 33–34, 43, 58, 67, 81–84
micro level xv, 9, 13, 33–34, 43, 67–68, 82–84, 92–95, 104–106
misalignment 89, 93–94
Moodle 25, 51

paradigm 15
pathways program 33–34, 86
pedagogy 10–12, 14, 39, 47, 104–105
policy 11, 33–34, 92–94, 97
power relations 51–52
principles 97–99
professional development 2, 18, 30–31, 39, 58, 75–76, 86, 96–97, 106
proficiency 24, 72, 79

quick fix 86

ramification 13, 27, 42, 65, 86, 106
repository 13, 25, 63, 70, 79
Royal College 16, 24–29, 33, 85–88, 91–95

scalability 7, 10, 32, 92, 97, 102
semi-structured interviews xiv, 70, 93
shared drive 49–50, 52, 72, 74
socio-cultural 33, 39, 58, 64, 85
Sony 2–3
stakeholders 10–11, 32–34, 81–83, 95–101
student engagement 10, 14–15, 63–64, 91
systems thinking 37–39

tablet computer 23–30, 33–35, 72–73
technology resistance 10, 30, 37, 53, 76–77, 92–94, 101
theory of change 99–103
timing 58–59
top-down 32, 68–69

uptake 2–4, 7, 33, 51, 77–78, 93–94
user-friendly 49

warrant 27, 33–34, 56–57, 96
workspace 78–79, 91, 102